truth in
science

because Worldview is essential

www.TRUTHINSCIENCE.com

Printed in Canada

Lesson 1

Introduce Plants

IN THIS UNIT, BE READY TO LEARN:

- The difference between worldviews when studying plants
- What a plant cell looks like and how it functions
- The functions of a plant's root and stem systems
- The suspect reasoning in the Evolutionary Tree of Life
- How plants get and use energy
- The growth process of plants
- How the fossil record is evidence of creation

VOCABULARY FOR THIS UNIT:

Epidermis—the thin outer layer of cells through which water and minerals from the soil enter the roots of plants

Xylem—part of a plant's vascular system that carries water and minerals to other parts of the plant

Phloem—part of a plant's vascular system that carries sugars throughout the plant

Tropism—plant behavior caused by growth toward or away from something in the environment

Guard cell—one of a pair of cells that work together to open and close a leaf's stoma

Transpiration—the loss of water from a leaf

Cellular respiration—the process by which cells combine glucose with oxygen for the release of energy

BEDROCK

To survive, plants have certain processes that allow them to live, grow and reproduce. God created mature plants on the third day of Creation complete with seeds.

Memory VERSE

Genesis 1:11

"Then God said, 'Let the earth bring forth grass, the herb that yields seed, and the fruit tree that yields fruit according to its kind, whose seed is in itself, on the earth'; and it was so."

STEP 1. When did God create plants? Read Genesis 1:11-13.

Genesis 1:11-13 "Then God said, 'Let the earth bring forth grass, the herb that yields seed, and the fruit tree that yields fruit according to its kind, whose seed is in itself, on the earth;' and it was so. And the earth brought forth grass, the herb that yields seed according to its kind. And God saw that it was good. So the evening and the morning were the third day."

1. When did God create plants?

_____

_____

_____

STEP 2. In the beginning, did God create seeds in the ground or full grown plants?

Have you ever heard the question, "Which came first, the chicken or the egg?" For nonbelievers, this can be a very hard question to answer. But for Believers, the answer is obvious and can be found in Genesis 1:21.

Which came first, the seed in the ground or trees with fruit? Genesis 1:11 says God created plants and trees that were seed-bearing.

Some of the trees may have looked like they were sixty, seventy, or a hundred years old, but they were not old. God created them as mature trees.

You will notice in the order of Creation that God made plants on the third day. He didn't make the sun until the fourth day. Plants need the light from the sun to live. If plants get life-giving energy from the light of the sun, how could they live without sun? Knowing that plants need the sun to live, we can safely assume that the days during Creation Week were 24 hours long, just like ours. A plant can live for one day without the sun.

2. In the beginning, did God create seeds in the ground or did He create full-grown plants?

_____

_____

_____

STEP 3. What do Evolutionists believe about the origin of plants?

Evolutionists believe life came from some non-living goo that existed at the bottom of the ocean. Somehow, that goo managed to arrange itself into simple marine animals. Then, a very long time later the simple marine animals arranged themselves into plants. Evolutionists believe that over eons of time, that goo became algae, ferns, and seed plants like flowers, vegetables, and fruit trees about 130 million years ago [hmmm, in lesson 6, evolutionists talk about the Wollemi pine fossil being 150 million years old. Do they have 30 million years in between these fossils?].

3. What do evolutionists believe about the origin of plants?

_____

_____

_____

Lesson 1 — Introduce Plants

STEP 4. Compare viewpoints of how plant life began.

Biblical Worldview—The Biblical worldview is that plants began on the third day of creation by God as mature plants complete with fruit and seeds.

Evolutionary Worldview—The Evolutionists' worldview is that plants evolved from non-living matter. After millions of years, there evolved fruit trees and other plants.

As you will see, the Evolutionary worldview believes that plants evolved from non-living matter (see the Evolution of Plants illustration in the above STEP 3); and, after millions of years, fruit trees and other plants evolved. Remember, also, that Evolutionists believe that marine animals evolved hundreds of millions of years before the evolution of fruit trees and other higher plants. But, the laws of science say that life can only come from life; life cannot come from something that is not alive. We will discuss this more in the Reproduction unit - Step 5.

The Biblical worldview, on the other hand, states in Genesis 1:11 that plants were created on the third day of Creation by the living God as mature plants complete with fruit and seeds. The Bible says God called forth (created) grass, plants, and trees. He didn't command that some simple life-forms such as bacteria or algae should come forth first. He didn't command that these life-forms should slowly change into other more complex plants over millions of years. No, the Bible says that the living God made plants as plants, trees as trees, and grass as grass on Day Three of Creation.

Creationists and Evolutionists look at the same data or evidence. In this case, we are examining the evidence of plant life from the past and plant life of today. However, Creationists and Evolutionists reach different conclusions because of their different worldviews or belief systems. Creationists believe God created plant life on Day Three of Creation. Evolutionists believe that living plants came from a nonliving substance, and it took millions of years for it to happen.

Directions:

1. From the vocabulary list, choose one word you would like to learn more about. Copy the word and its definition in the "I know" box.

2. What would you like to learn more about this word? Write your questions in the "I Wonder" box.

3. As you study this chapter, be aware of the answer to your questions.

4. At the end of the chapter, fill in the box "I learned."

I KNOW...

_____

_____

_____

I WONDER...

_____

_____

_____

I LEARNED...

_____

_____

_____

_____

Lesson 1

Vocabulary

Directions: Match the correct word to the definition by writing the letter of the word in the circle.

Letter	Definition	Word
◯	1. the loss of water from a leaf	A. epidermis
◯	2. part of a plant's vascular system that carries water and minerals to other parts of the plants	B. xylem
◯	3. the process by which cells combine glucose with oxygen for the release of energy	C. phloem
◯	4. one of a pair of cells that work together to open and close a leaf's stoma	D. tropism
◯	5. the thin outer layer of plant cells through which water and minerals from the soil enter the roots	E. guard cell
◯	6. part of a plant's vascular system that carries sugars throughout the plant	F. transpiration
◯	7. plant behavior caused by growth toward or away from something in the environment	G. cellular respiration

Project: Plants in the Bible

This project will be due at the end of this Step, before the tests.

What Do I Want to Know?

This project will enable you to learn about plants discussed in the Bible, while reviewing plant vocabulary.

What Materials Do I Need?

- A computer with Internet access and/or other research materials.
- A word processor.

How Will I Do It?

1. Visit http://christiananswers.net/dictionary/plants.html and choose a plant to report on.

2. After choosing your plant, use the Internet and/or reference books to further investigate and research.

3. Pretend you are a plant salesman. Create a brochure advertising your plant. Include your research in your brochure, answering the following:

   — What was the relevance of the plant in Scripture?

   — Is the plant an angiosperm or gymnosperm?

   — Is the plant an annual, biannual or perennial?

4. Include pictures and other relevant information about your plant.

5. Share your results.

   — Answer any questions about the steps.

   — Work independently or at home on this activity. If this is a group activity, plan class time to work in teams.

   — Brainstorm over solutions to any problems or issues that may be perceived as obstacles. Encourage problem-solving.

How Did I Do?

Your score will be determined by the following criteria:

- Project Visuals (20 points)
  — Scientific Accuracy
  — Completed according to directions
  — Neatness
- Written Report (20 points)
  — Completed according to directions
  — Neatness
- Project Creativity (20 points)
- Oral Presentation (20 points)
  — Eye contact
  — Voice Projection
  — Confidence in material
- Worldview Accuracy (20 points)

Consider the Wonder

Consider: What is a Plant Cell?

Cells are what living things are made of, and we often call them the building blocks of living things. So, a plant cell is the building block of plants. Each plant that you see is made up of millions of these tiny cells all working together. When studying living things (except for bacteria), scientists sort most cells into two major groups: Plant cells and Animal cells.

All cells have a cell membrane which acts as a boundary to keep all of the cell's contents inside. In addition to the cell membrane, plant cells also have a special layer called the cell wall. The cell wall of the plant cells in this demonstration will be easy to see through the microscope. This cell wall makes the plant rigid (stiff) and gives the plant structure. As you will see, each one of the plant cells looks rectangular. The cell wall helps keep these cells from flattening or changing their shape, which helps the plant to grow strong.

Prepare

This activity serves as an introduction to plant cells and their functions. In this activity you will observe the cells of an onion skin. Before looking conducting the lab, ask yourself the following question: What do you think a cell looks like? Make a prediction and record your answer in the Science Journal.

Before you begin this lab, you may visit the website below to conduct a mini-research. Websites you may wish to visit are: www.cellsalive.com and/or www.eurekascience.com/ICanDoThat/plant_cells.htm

What You Will Need:

- Piece of onion skin
- Tincture of Iodine and/or bromthymol blue
- Slides
- Cover slips
- Water dropper
- Microscope
- Internet Access

What to Do

- With the help of an adult, prepare the slides for viewing before you begin the activity. Using tweezers and maybe a razor blade or exacto knife, extract a piece of the thin tissue located between the layers of an onion.
- Float the tissue on top of water in a shallow pan.
- Slide the microscope slide under the tissue and slowly lift it out of the water. Make sure the specimen is smaller than the coverslip.
- Place the coverslip over the tissue (there will be a little water left) and slowly allow it to "fall" over the tissue, as in a door closing.
- Put a drop of iodine or bromthymol blue right next to the coverslip. This will suck right into the onion skin, giving a very clear look at the cells in the skin.
- Observe the plant cell under the microscope.
- Draw your observations and answer the following questions.

What Did You Find?

- What does the cell of a plant look like?
- What do you suppose is the function of a plant cell?

In the space provided make a Science Journal entry answering one of the questions from the activity. Were your predictions of what would happen correct? What did you observe? What could be done differently to change the results?

Predictions: (I think)

Observations: (I saw, felt, heard or smelled)

Conclusions: (I found out)

Lesson 3

Vascular Plants

STEP 1. Read Job 18:16. How important is the root system to the rest of the plant?

Job 18:16 "His roots are dried out below, and his branch withers above."

Even though the Bible is not a "science book," any time that it talks about science, it is always correct. The Book of Job contains many references to science that are true. This lesson's Bible verse in Job 18:16 is an example of true science expressed in the Bible.

Reflect: Do you think Job conducted a scientific investigation on the root system of plants to know that when the roots are dried out that the rest of the plant (in this case the branches) will die? Or, do you think he was given this information another way? How would you test this observation about dried roots?

In vascular plants, the leaves manufacture food for the plant, but they need water and nutrients for the process to work. The root system is how the water and nutrients are transported (moved) to the rest of the plant. The roots absorb the water from the ground, and the water then moves to the rest of the plant. But, if the roots are withered up (dried up), they cannot provide the necessary water for the plant to produce its own food and it will die. Also, without proper root formation, the leaves will probably not form properly; and, if they do, they will quickly die. Strong roots are very important for the life of the plant.

Reflect: Matthew 13:5-6, 20-21a, is another place in the Bible where the importance of roots is mentioned.

Matthew 13:5-6, 20-21a "Some [seeds] fell on stony places, where they did not have much earth; and they immediately sprang up because they had no depth of earth. But when the sun was up they were scorched, and because they had no root they withered away....

But he who received the seed on stony places, this is he who hears the word and immediately receives it with joy; yet he has no root in himself, but endures only for a while."

Why do you think the plants "immediately sprang up"? These seeds were spread on rocky soil so there wasn't a deep layer of dirt that the plants had to come up through. Therefore, they grew quickly and did not have a strong root system. But what happened when the bright sun was shining? Since their roots were not very deep in the dirt, the sun dried them out and the plant died because the roots could not draw water from the ground and distribute nutrients to the plant. This passage is an example of a scientific truth within the Bible.

1. Read Job 18:16. How important is the root system to the rest of the plant?

Job 18:16 "His roots are dried out below, and his branch withers above."

_____

_____

_____

STEP 2. The Bible says that before Adam and Eve sinned, there was no death, disease, or suffering. If Adam ate a carrot, does that mean the Bible is wrong since a plant obviously had to die?

When God created the world, He created a perfect world. Adam and Eve were perfect in every way. God's creation was "very good," and He said so (Genesis 1:31). There was no death, disease, or suffering before Adam and Eve disobeyed God in the garden of Eden. We refer to this time of disobedience as the "Fall," and after that time, their life became difficult. Adam and Eve's disobedience brought sin, death and suffering into the world. The Apostle Paul talks about man's fall in his letter to the

Romans: "Therefore, just as through one man sin entered the world, and death through sin, and thus death spread to all men..." (5:12). Paul emphasizes that death is a consequence of sin. Before sin entered the world by man's disobedience, there was no death.

In our studies, we have examined the evolutionary definition of life (it just "happened" from non-life) and the Biblical definition of life (God created life). During your lifetime, you will meet people who will say the Bible is wrong and that God did not and could not create life. So, how could you answer these people? Let's think about the following question: Do plants have Biblical life?

Remember our study of the Hebrew word ruach in the Classification Step? Do plants have ruach (breath)? Do they breathe air, like animals? No, plants do not breathe like animals--they don't have lungs, and they don't use oxygen the same way animals do. They have an exchange of gases--carbon dioxide and oxygen. Animals don't make oxygen, they only use oxygen.

In the Classification Step, we also studied the Hebrew word dam. Do plants have dam (blood)? Do plants have blood that flows throughout their tissues like animals? The purpose of blood in animals is to supply nutrition to all the cells of the body—water, vitamins, minerals, and other things. Vascular plants—plants with veins called xylem and phloem—move nutrients, but it is not to every cell. The type of substance found in plants that is most like blood is an oxygen-carrying substance that is found only in the roots. It does not match the Biblical definition of dam.

The Bible makes a very clear distinction between the physical state of plants and animals. Plants do not have ruach (breath) and plants do not have dam (blood). Therefore, plants do not meet the Biblical definition of life.

2. The Bible says that before Adam and Eve sinned, there was no death, disease, or suffering.

If Adam ate a carrot, does that mean the Bible is wrong since a plant obviously had to die? Why or why not?

_____

_____

_____

STEP 3. Movement in man and animals is accomplished by the muscle system. Similarities of movement in animals and plants have been used as "proof" of the evolution of animals FROM plants. What can the similarities strongly suggest?

Evolutionists sometimes try to prove that animals evolved FROM plants by comparing them to each other. They say that there are two movements within a plant's structure that look like they might be like animals. They think this supports evolution of plants to animals. The physical movement that Evolutionists compare this to in humans and animals is that of the muscles in the skeletal system.

The first movement in their argument is the movement of the guard cells that work together to open and close the leaf's stoma. In plants, the guard cells allow oxygen, carbon dioxide, and water to pass through the stoma. This movement is accomplished by the guard cells' absorption of water. When the guard cell swells, it bulges and pushes outward to create the opening for the stoma to release the gases or water, or to take in the gas.

But, this movement is actually OPPOSITE of the way the skeletal system functions within the muscle system in man and animals. In man and animals, the muscles work by contracting and opposing each other against the skeleton. In the stomates (the openings), the water expanding does all the action, and the tissues of the plants receive the benefit.

The second movement is the rise of sap up the trunk of a tree, or the movement of nutrients—water,

Lesson 3

Vascular Plants

minerals, sugar—through the veins of the vascular plant's xylem and phloem. The nutrients (water, minerals and sugar) are moved within the plant because of cohesion (the attribute of sticking together). The water molecules stick together. By evaporation and osmosis, it is pulled to the topmost point of the plants. No one can observe the movement of the sap through the tree; but, a contracting muscle is certainly not squeezing the sap up the tree. There is no connection or similarity between the movement of nutrients in plants and muscle function in humans and animals.

The movements observed in plants do not prove evolution. It does not make the link that muscles evolved from a plant's vascular system. There is no evidence found anywhere of this strange morphing of one Kingdom to another. What it does show is that any common needs for form and function call for common structures by a common designer.

All organisms (man, animals, and plants) have some common needs. A good designer will use some of the same basic design features for all His work. If it works in one situation, it will work in another.

3. Movement in man and animals is accomplished by the muscle system. Similarities of movement in animals and plants have been used as "proof" of the evolution of animals FROM plants. What can the similarities strongly suggest? Fill in the blank.

Common _____ for form and function call for common _____ by a common _____.

Let's begin our study of vascular plants from the bottom at the root system and work our way out through the leaves.

2. Science Instruction

- The root system has two purposes: One purpose is to anchor the plant in place and another purpose is to take in minerals and water from the soil that will be transported to the rest of the plant.

- Vascular plants have tubes that transport nutrients throughout the plant.

- Xylem moves water and minerals from the roots to the other parts of a plant.

- Phloem moves sugar from the leaves to other parts of a plant.

- The purpose of a plant's stems is to give the plant support and transport materials between the roots and leaves.

- Plants can be herbaceous or woody.

- The plant's food is a sugar called glucose.

- Gases (oxygen and carbon dioxide) and water pass through small openings in the leaves called stoma. Two guard cells work together to open and close the leaf's stoma.

- Water will exit a plant's leaves through a process called transpiration (this is simply "evaporation from the surface of a living thing"--skin in animals transpires, too). The air temperature, wind, and the amount of water in the air and soil will affect how much water is lost during transpiration.

Science Review

Directions: Choose a word from the word bank to complete the following sentences.

1. The purpose of a plant's roots is to _____ the plant in place and to take in _____ and _____ from the soil.

2. Plants that have tubes that transport nutrients throughout the plant are called _____ plants. Water and minerals are moved from the roots to the other parts of a plant by the _____. Sugar moves from the leaves to other parts of a plant by the _____.

3. The purpose of a plant's _____ is to give the plant support and transport materials between the roots and leaves.

4. Plants can be _____ or woody.

5. The plant's food is a sugar called _____.

6. Gas (oxygen and carbon dioxide) and water pass through small openings in the leaves called _____. Two _____ cells work together to open and close the leaf's stoma.

7. Water is lost from a plant's leaves through a process called _____. The air temperature, wind, and the amount of water in the air and soil will affect how much water is lost.

Word Bank

anchor	transpiration	vascular	stems	glucose	xylem
phloem	minerals	stoma	guard	water	herbaceous

Lesson 4
How Plants Get and Use Energy

STEP 1. Photosynthesis is the chemical process that plants use to change energy from the sun into their food. There is a lot about photosynthesis that scientists don't understand. What is one thing they do understand?

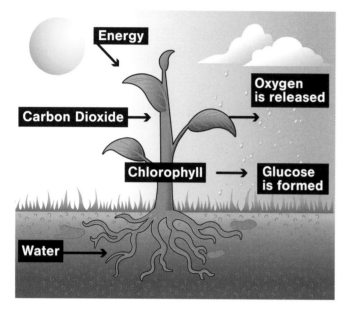

Photosynthesis is the marvelous process a plant uses to make its food. During photosynthesis, the plant takes energy from the sun, carbon dioxide from the air, water, and minerals from the cell, and combines them with chlorophyll to produce glucose (sugar) for its food. It also produces oxygen as a by-product. (Chlorophyll is the green pigment, or coloring, in plants.)

Numerous scientists have studied and conducted research on photosynthesis for more than 100 years and only recently have they begun to understand the process. However, there is still much to learn. One thing we do know: It is a very complicated process.

1. Photosynthesis is the chemical process that plants use to change energy from the sun into their food. There is a lot about photosynthesis that scientists don't understand. What is one thing they do understand?

_____

_____

_____

STEP 2. If we cannot use the energy directly from the sun, how can we get energy indirectly from the sun?

During the week of Creation, God created the heavens and the earth. It was not until Day 4 that He created the sun. The light energy for those first three days came directly from God, who is light. He created the sun to be a light-holder of His energy.

We need energy. We cannot use the energy directly from the sun, so how can we get energy?

Green plants absorb energy from the sun and use it to make their food. We, in turn, eat the plants and use it for our energy. Or, we eat animals that have eaten green plants, and we get energy from them.

Plants are an example of God's creativity and power. They take light energy, combine it with minerals and water from the earth and molecules in the air, and create chemical energy. This energy is made available to us in the form of plants for us and the animals to eat. It has kept men and animals alive since the beginning of creation.

2. If we cannot use the energy directly from the sun, how can we get energy indirectly from the sun?

_____

_____

_____

STEP 3. Why would photosynthesis have had to have been in place from the beginning and not be a product of evolution?

Photosynthesis could not have evolved because it needs energy to begin the photosynthesis. But that energy also is made by photosynthesis.

All of life is dependent on energy that comes from the sun. In Lesson 3, you learned that photosynthesis is the process that captures the energy from the sun and converts it into the kind of energy (chemical energy) that can be used by living things. (See Vascular Plants and Could Photosynthesis Have Evolved? illustrations.) Life as we know it could not exist without photosynthesis.

Photosynthesis requires complex processes right from the start. It is what Dr. Michael Behe would describe as irreducible complexity--it cannot operate to sustain life without all of its parts and systems intact. Simply stated, irreducible complexity means that something cannot function until all of its parts are together. An often used example is that of a mousetrap. If the mousetrap is missing just one of its parts, the mousetrap will not work. All the parts must be there from the beginning, allowing no time for evolution to occur.

3. Why would photosynthesis had to have been in place from the beginning and not evolved? Fill in the blanks.

Photosynthesis could not have evolved because it

needs _____ to begin the _____.

2. Science Instruction

- Through the process of photosynthesis, plants make glucose (sugar).

- Photosynthesis (the process of capturing energy from the sun and converting it into energy) takes place in the chloroplasts of the leaf cells of plants. Look at the illustration and locate the tall, thin cells in the middle of the leaf. Note their tall, rectangular shape. This is where most of the sunlight is absorbed. These thin cells also contain the green chloroplasts that are needed to make sugar.

- Chlorophyll is contained in the chloroplasts. (Chlorophyll is what gives plants their green color.)

- Leaves have many features that participate in the function of performing photosynthesis. Look at the illustration and identify two functions that leaves have in photosynthesis.

- All organisms, plants and animals, must break down food to release the stored energy. The illustration shows that organisms take in oxygen and glucose, and then release carbon dioxide, energy, and water. This process is called cellular respiration.

- Cellular respiration takes place in the mitochondria of cells.

- Photosynthesis and cellular respiration are reverse processes of each other (photosynthesis makes food that will be used for energy in cellular respiration):

- Photosynthesis is: light energy + carbon dioxide + water → chemical energy + oxygen. The light energy is from the sun and the chemical energy is in the form of the sugar, glucose.

- Cellular respiration is: chemical energy + oxygen → carbon dioxide + water. The chemical energy is from the food we eat, often as glucose and other sugars.

Lesson 4

How Plants Get and Use Energy

Science Review

Directions: Choose a word from the word bank to complete the following sentences.

1. Through the process of photosynthesis, plants make _____.

2. Photosynthesis takes place in the _____ of the leaf cells of plants. Chlorophyll is contained in these organelles.

3. Leaves have many _____ that participate in the function of performing photosynthesis.

4. All organisms, plants and animals, must break down food to release the _____ energy. This process is called _____ _____.

5. Photosynthesis and cellular respiration are _____ processes of each other.

6. Photosynthesis is: light energy → carbon dioxide → water → chemical energy → oxygen. The light energy is from the sun and the _____ energy is in the form of the sugar, glucose.

7. Cellular respiration is: chemical energy → oxygen → _____ _____ → water. The chemical energy is from the food we eat, often as glucose, other sugars, or fats and starches.

Word Bank

features	chloroplasts	stored	chemical	carbon dioxide
reverse	glucose	cellular	respiration	

STEP 1. What is the feature of plants that causes them to respond to their environment and is often used by Evolutionists as evidence for evolution?

Sometimes living things, such as plants, have been observed to change according to the environment in which they live. For example, mountaintops are dry and rocky because they are windy and water runs off the mountain. Therefore, trees on the tops of mountains are short and gnarly (twisted). Valleys, however, are protected from the wind, and the water from the mountaintops runs into the valley providing water for the trees. Trees in a valley generally grow tall and straight. Evolutionary scientists suggest that environmental changes resulted in permanent changes and the creation of a new species. Is this true? Could these kinds of changes ever create a new species? Or, are they the result of natural selection? This kind of activity would more accurately be called natural selection and is not the same as biological evolution.

To understand why this is not macro-evolution (evolution outside of the Biblical kind), one must understand a little about DNA (Deoxyribonucleic acid), the instruction code of the plant's cells.

Cells are the building blocks of life. Within every cell are instructions for that cell's job. In an organism, every cell's set of instructions are the same. The only difference is some instructions are turned off and some are turned on depending upon which job in the body each cell is doing. This set of instructions is called DNA.

As an example, imagine a field of Black-Eyed Susans growing in abundance on a Maryland hillside. Now suppose that the weather in Maryland, which had cycled through several rainy years, was now cycling through a serious drought. Observers of the Black-Eyed Susans would notice that after several growing seasons, the Black-Eyed Susans would have developed longer roots and a waxier coating on the leaves. The longer roots would give them better

access to water at the deeper levels. The waxier coating on the leaves would prevent the plants from losing too much moisture through transpiration.

The instruction set for the Black-Eyed Susans contained the information for deeper roots and waxier coatings. When the environment became dry, the DNA "turned on" the instructions for the roots to grow deeper to find water, and for the leaves to be more coated to prevent the loss of water from the leaves. These plants adapted to survive in their surroundings. This could not have happened without the instructions already having been in the DNA. Variations are not the same as macro-evolution. Variations make changes in individuals, not new species. The Black-Eyed Susans are still Black-Eyed Susans. Macro-evolution would have required new information to appear that was not already there.

One can only suppose that if the Black-Eyed Susans had been observed during the rainy years, there would have been some plants with long roots, short roots, medium roots, waxy coatings, and less waxy coatings. That is because every population has a distinct, built-in variety. (For instance, just look around the room at the different eyebrows and ears.) As the environment began to experience the drier conditions, the plants with the short roots and less waxy coatings died out without reproducing. Only the Black-Eyed Susans with longer roots and waxier coatings would have survived. This is called natural selection.

Natural selection is the term used to describe the superiority of a certain combination of instructions over another. This superiority is determined by the environmental conditions. However, this selection process only reacts to the instructions that already exist in the organism. It will not be able to create more complex or new information. It cannot become a new species. Adaptations and natural selection are not evolution.

1. What is the feature of plants that causes them

Lesson 5

How Plants Grow

to respond to their environment and is often used by Evolutionists as evidence to support their model?

_____

_____

_____

2. Science Instruction

- Plants that produce seeds in flowers (flowering plants) are vascular plants called angiosperms.

- Plants that produce seeds in cones are called gymnosperms.

- To germinate, all seeds need water, oxygen, and a certain temperature.

- Some plants don't grow from seeds. They grow from spores instead.

- Most plants get larger by producing new cells at the tips of the roots and stems. Some plants have growth that increases a plant's width. Branches grow from side buds.

- A plant grows in different directions in response to environmental conditions. This turning is called tropism. Growing away from gravity is called geotropism. Growing toward the light is called phototropism.

⑤ Seeds are scattered by wind, water and animals.

① Seed begins to germinate.

② Root grows down; stem pushes up.

④ Plant makes flowers and seeds.

③ Leaves begin to grow and make food for the plant.

Leaves make sugar and oxygen.

Leaves use water, carbon dioxide, and energy from sunlight.

TRUTH IN SCIENCE: BECAUSE WORLDVIEW IS ESSENTIAL

Science Review

Directions: Choose a word from the word bank to complete the following sentences.

1. Plants that produce seeds in _____ are vascular plants called angiosperms.

2. Plants that produce seeds in _____ are called gymnosperms.

3. To germinate, all seeds need _____, _____ and a certain _____.

4. Some plants don't grow from seeds. They grow from _____ instead.

5. Most plants get larger by producing new cells at the _____ of the roots and stems. Some plants have growth that increases a plant's _____. Branches grow from side buds.

6. A plant grows in different directions in response to environmental conditions. This turning is called _____.

Word Bank

temperature	oxygen	cones	water	environmental
flowers	width	tips	spores	tropism

Lesson 6

Comparing Plants from the Past

STEP 1. What is missing in the evolution of plants?

You will recall from Lesson 1 that Evolutionists believe plants began as non-living matter in the bottom of a body of water. Then, over a very long period of time, the non-living matter slowly changed from one form to another to become the complex plants and trees that we see today. Evolutionists say that some of the earliest plants did not have flowers or cones. They believe that these "plants" evolved into coniferous trees. Then these trees evolved into flowering plants. They base these assumptions (guesses) on the evidence found in rock layers. They also assume that the lower the level of rock, the older the age of the rock. Evolutionists don't believe that there was a global Flood. Therefore, they have to assume that it took millions of years to form each rock layer. Creationists, however, believe it could have happened in few months, days, hours, or even minutes, under the waters of Noah's Flood.

What is one problem with this idea? If one form of plants evolved or slowly changed into another, there should be fossil evidence in the rock layers. Remember, the rock layers are what the Evolutionists use as evidence to support their model of millions of years. According to the evolutionary model, simple plants evolved into complex plants. Mosses (nonseed-bearing plants) became small seed-bearing plants, and those eventually became flowers and trees. If that were true, scientists who study fossils should have discovered many fossils of plants that were changing from seed-bearing plants into flowering plants. There should be some in-between forms of plants in the rocks. But there are none. Why not? These in-between forms are called missing links.

To believe in the evolution of plants, one must be able to imagine what an ancestor of flowering plants might have looked like. Since no one was around to see evolution happen, one must take a blind leap of "evolutionary" faith to believe how it happened. That is, one would have to imagine how the intricate, detailed flowers that we see today modified

(re-organized) themselves to be specialized for reproduction. However, there is no fossil evidence of any kind to support this remarkable "leap" from nonseed-bearing plants to seed-bearing plants. For a leaf to have morphed or changed into an ovary (female) or pollen (male) would have required new information to have been added to the DNA of the cell. What is true, is that in the very beginning, all the information for a given plant was created with a complete instruction set for leaves, stems, and specialized parts.

1. What is missing in the evolution of plants?

_____

_____

STEP 2. Does the "dinosaur tree" seem to support Creation or evolution?

In 1994, a living Wollemi Pine was discovered in a remote canyon in Australia, and it was dubbed "the Dinosaur Tree." The Dinosaur Tree is considered a "living fossil" because it had long been thought to be extinct since the Jurassic Age approximately 150 million years ago. However, this "living fossil" is an organism that is practically unchanged from fossils that are supposedly 150 million years old. According to evolution, its form should have had significant changes by this time, if it is that old. This fact suggests that the vast ages of time are questionable.

The reason these trees are here today is because these trees are from today's world, and not from millions of years ago. If the Dinosaur Tree was a prehistoric tree, it would not be here today for us to study it.

The current Wollemi Pine has changed little, if any, compared to its fossil which is supposedly millions of years old. If evolution were real, wouldn't there have been a change by now?

2. Does the "dinosaur tree" seem to support creation or evolution? Why?

_____

_____

_____

STEP 3. Scientists have found plant spores buried deeper in earth's rock layers than ever before. How are some evolutionists explaining the new evidence?

Evolutionists believe that the layers of rock indicate geological time. The term "geological time" means the length of time it supposedly took for the rock layers to be laid down. They think that the different rock layers were slowly and systematically laid down over millions of years. Evolutionists also believe that plant and animal fossils found in the rock layers are indicators of the stage of an organism's evolution. In the evolution of plants, they believe that land plants which reproduce from spores (like mosses and ferns) evolved from water plants like algae. Recently, they have found some new data. They have found spores in rock that would push the origin of land plants back tens of millions of years earlier than they had previously thought. This information creates a problem for their evolutionary model.

Because they are having a hard time reconciling the evolutionary times to the rock evidence, they are beginning to think that maybe the spores came to Earth from outer space. Maybe a meteor or comet

crashed on the earth carrying these spores. The only evidence they have is spores in the rock layers. They do not have spores in meteors or comets. They are imagining that is what may have happened. The conclusion of how the spores got in the rock layers depends on a person's worldview. One might wonder why some people can believe in life from outer space, but they won't believe a global flood covered the whole world about 4,300 years ago.

3. Scientists have found plant spores buried deeper in earth's rock layers than ever before. How are some evolutionists explaining the new evidence?

_____

_____

_____

2. Science Instruction

- Scientists learn about plants that lived long ago by studying fossils.

- Fossils of plants form in three ways.

- The first way is when an impression of a plant part is made in soft mud that hardens and turns into rock.

- The second way is when rock or mineral material replaces the parts of a plant over a long period of time, like in a petrified tree.

- The third is when a plant gets trapped flat between rock layers, and everything but the element carbon gets squeezed out by the pressure, and the carbon leaves what looks like a black shadow in the rock.

- Plants within a group may change over time, but they are still similar to plants in their group from long ago. This supports Creation and the command from God for plants to make more plants according to their various kinds.

Lesson 6
Comparing Plants from the Past

Science Review

Directions: Choose a word from the word bank to complete the following sentences.

1. Scientists learn about plants that lived long ago by studying _____.

2. Fossils of plants form in three ways. The first way is when an impression of a plant part is made in soft _____ that later turns into rock. The second way is when rock or mineral material _____ the parts of a plant over a long period of time, like in a petrified tree. The third way is when a plant gets trapped flat between rock layers and everything but the element carbon gets squeezed out by the pressure, the carbon leaves what looks like a black shadow in the rock.

3. Plants within a group may change over time, but they are still _____ to plants in their group from long ago. This _____ Creation and the command from God for plants to make more plants according to their various kinds.

Word Bank

mud	fossils	similar	replaces	supports

Inquire: How Does Water Travel in a Flower?

This activity demonstrates how water travels through plant stems to bring food and nutrients to all parts of a flower. When you water a plant, where does the water go? How will the water get nutrients to all parts of a plant?

Time Required: 10-15 minutes to set up, 10-15 minutes for observation (after 2-24 hours).

Make a Prediction: After you set up your experiment, ask yourself the following questions: Which color will reach the petals first? Will the combination make a new color? Next, make a prediction in your Science Journal about what you think you will observe at the end of the experiment.

What You Need

- 3 white carnations (for each group)
- 5 plastic cups (for each group)
- Water
- Food coloring (5 colors)
- Knife or scalpel

What You Will Do

- Fill each cup halfway with water and put 20-30 drops of food coloring in each. **Remember that food coloring will stain, so use caution.**
- Trim each flower by cutting the stem at an angle. It is best to cut the flower under running water to prevent air bubbles from traveling up the stem.
- Place one of the carnations in one cup of water and predict how long it might take for the colored water to reach the petals.

- **Ask an adult to help you slice the carnations.** For the remaining two carnations, use the knife to slice the stems right down the middle. Place one-half of each stem into a cup of water. Use different colors for each half.
- Check back every few hours to observe how the color has spread. Be sure to check all parts of the flower for traces of color (petals, stem, buds, leaves, etc.)
- Discuss the results in your science journal.

What Happened?

- How did the water travel from the cup to the parts of the flower?
- How do the roots and stems contribute to plant growth?

What Now?

- What did you learn about the function of stems?
- How might chemicals or pollutants in the soil and water affect plant growth?
- Write one or two paragraphs in the Science Journal summarizing your findings and explaining what you learned. Were your predictions of what would happen correct? What did you observe? What could be done differently to change the results?

Science Journal

In the space provided make a Science Journal entry answering one of the questions from the activity. Were your predictions of what would happen correct? What did you observe? What could be done differently to change the results?

Predictions: (I think)

Observations: (I saw, felt, heard or smelled)

Conclusions: (I found out)

Project: Plants in the Bible
What Do I Want to Know?

This project will enable you to learn about plants discussed in the Bible, while reviewing plant vocabulary.

What Materials Do I Need?

- A computer with Internet access and/or other research materials.
- A word processor.

How Will I Do It?

1. Visit http://christiananswers.net/dictionary/plants.html and choose a plant to report on.

2. After choosing your plant, use the Internet and/or reference books to further investigate and research.

3. Pretend you are a plant salesman. Create a brochure advertising your plant. Include your research in your brochure, answering the following:

   — What was the relevance of the plant in Scripture?

   — Is the plant an angiosperm or gymnosperm?

   — Is the plant an annual, biannual or perennial?

4. Include pictures and other relevant information about your plant.

5. Share your results.

   — Answer any questions about the steps.

   — Assign students to work independently or at home on this activity. If this is a group activity, plan class time for students to work in teams.

   — Brainstorm with students over solutions to any problems or issues that may be perceived as obstacles. Encourage problem-solving.

How Did I Do?

Your score will be determined by the following criteria:

- Project Visuals (20 points)
  - Scientific Accuracy
  - Completed according to directions
  - Neatness
- Written Report (20 points)
  - Completed according to directions
  - Neatness
- Project Creativity (20 points)
- Oral Presentation (20 points)
  - Eye contact
  - Voice Projection
  - Confidence in material
- Worldview Accuracy (20 points)

Schedule a time with your teacher for the presentation of your report.

Democracy, Law, and Justice

BY DANIEL S. CAMPAGNA, Ph. D., AND ANN BEAUCHAMP CAMPAGNA

Copyright © 1996 Mark Twain Media, Inc.

ISBN 1–58037–006–3

Printing No. CD–1860

Mark Twain Media, Inc., Publishers
Distributed by Carson-Dellosa Publishing Company, Inc.

Table of Contents

Introduction

The purpose of this book is to provide the reader with a general understanding of our judicial system and how it functions within a democratic society. To that end, we shall examine the many people, events, agencies, and concepts that comprise the criminal justice system of the United States.

To better acquaint the reader with this knowledge, a number of study aids are included. All terms are clearly defined and highlighted. Practical examples are given to illustrate how such terms are applied in the judicial process. Case studies, hypotheses, and "what-if" scenarios challenge the readers' imaginations. Current statistical data on crime and justice gives an accurate interpretation of the crime problem in America. Lastly, a diverse and ample range of problem-solving exercises are incorporated as standard features of each chapter. These activities stimulate critical thinking and arouse curiosity as to how the judicial system functions.

At the conclusion of this book, the reader shall have a broad working knowledge of law, justice, and democracy. Also, this information will be of direct benefit to those interested in the basic structure and principles of American government. The chapters are connected by a single theme known as "the rule of law." In order to exist, our judicial system requires the rule of law. In order to function as a democracy, our government is based on the rule of law. How the judicial system and the government coexist under the rule of law is the focus of this book.

—*THE AUTHORS*

United States Constitution

The *Constitution* is the single most important document in our nation's history. Delegates of the Constitutional Convention met in 1787 in Philadelphia to draft a workable constitution for their new government. It was originally composed of a *preamble* and seven *articles*. Since its creation, 27 *amendments* have been added to it. The first ten of these amendments are known as the *Bill of Rights.*

In a sense, the Constitution is our government, since it provides the essential set of guidelines for an orderly society that our nation is based on. The Constitution is the chief authority on every issue having to do with rights, freedoms, and the powers of government and people. We turn to it for solutions in sorting out the problems common to a democracy. What, for instance, are the rights of a citizen who makes a racist remark in public?

Also, keep in mind that the Constitution is a "living" document, open to change. Each of the 27 amendments seeks to clarify or modify some point of the Constitution. Naturally, the delegates could not have foreseen the needs of, or changes in, society in the future. Thus, the amendments serve a necessary role in keeping our Constitution relevant through changing times. The nineteenth amendment of 1920 is a practical case in point. It upholds the right of any female citizen of the United States to vote. Prior to passage of the nineteenth amendment, women were barred from voting. The amendment, therefore, promoted equality of voting rights (suffrage) for women. By periodically "updating" the Constitution through court decisions, laws, and amendments, we help preserve its basic strength as the foundation of our nation.

The framers of the Constitution expected it to endure and withstand the tests of time. Since the Bill of Rights, only 17 amendments have been added to it. The U.S. Constitution is the oldest written constitution in the world. It created a three-tiered system of government—executive, legislative, and judicial—that has successfully weathered grave threats such as the Civil War, presidential assassinations, and Watergate. This strength in the face of adversity may explain why many other nations have created their own written constitutions that are in many ways similar to the U.S. Constitution.

"If men were angels, no government would be necessary. If angels were to govern men, neither external or internal controls would be necessary. In framing a government which is to be administered by men over men, the great difficulty lies in this; you must first enable the government to control the governed; and then in the next place oblige it to control itself."

-*James Madison*-

Name _____ Date _____

Preamble to the United States Constitution

"We the people of the United States, in order to form a more perfect union, establish justice, insure domestic tranquility, provide for the common defense, promote the general welfare, and secure the blessings of liberty to ourselves and our posterity, do ordain and establish this Constitution for the United States of America."

1. What were some of the things that the founding fathers (those who wrote the constitution) tried to guarantee in the constitution?

_____

_____

_____

2. The United States Constitution is over 200 years old. If it were being written today, what ideals do you think we would try to promote?

_____

_____

_____

On Your Own:

Write a 21st century preamble to the United States Constitution.

_____

_____

_____

_____

_____

_____

_____

Bill of Rights

The first ten amendments to the United States Constitution are known as the Bill of Rights. They describe, in broad terms, many of our essential rights and freedoms. Over time, the courts have tried to clarify the extent and precise meaning of these amendments.

Amendment 1:   Congress shall make no law respecting an establishment of religion, or prohibiting the free exercise thereof; or abridging the freedom of speech, or of the press; or the right of the people peaceably to assemble, and to petition the Government for a redress of grievances.

Summary: **Freedom of religion, speech, press, assembly, and to petition the government.**

Amendment 2:   A well-regulated militia, being necessary to the security of a free State, the right of the people to keep and bear arms, shall not be infringed.

Summary: **Right to keep and bear arms.**

Amendment 3:   No Soldier shall, in time of peace be quartered in any house, without the consent of the owner, nor in time of war, but in a manner to be prescribed by law.

Summary: **Soldiers cannot be placed in homes without owners' consent.**

Amendment 4:   The right of the people to be secure in their persons, houses, papers, and effects, against unreasonable searches and seizures, shall not be violated, and no warrants shall issue, but upon probable cause, supported by oath or affirmation, and particularly describing the place to be searched, and the persons or things to be seized.

Summary: **Security from unreasonable searches and seizures; probable cause needed for warrants.**

Amendment 5:   No person shall be held to answer for a capital, or otherwise infamous crime, unless on a presentment or indictment of a Grand Jury, except in cases arising in the land or naval forces, or in the militia, when in actual service in time of war or public danger; nor shall any person be subject for the same offense to be twice put in jeopardy of life or limb; nor shall be compelled in any criminal case to be a witness against himself, nor be deprived of life, liberty, or property, without due process of law; nor shall private property be taken for public use, without just compensation.

Summary: **No self incrimination or double jeopardy for crimes; right to a grand jury, due process of law, and compensation for taking of public property.**

7

Amendment 6:   In all criminal prosecutions, the accused shall enjoy the right to a speedy and public trial, by an impartial jury of the State and district wherein the crime shall have been committed, which district shall have been previously ascertained by law, and to be informed of the nature and cause of the accusation; to be confronted with the witnesses against him; to have compulsory process for obtaining witnesses in his favor, and to have the assistance of counsel for his defense.

Summary: **Right to a speedy trial by jury, to be informed of charges, confront witnesses, and have legal advice.**

Amendment 7:   In suits at common law, where the value in controversy shall exceed twenty dollars, the right of trial by jury shall be preserved, and no fact tried by a jury, shall be otherwise reexamined in any Court of the United States, than according to the rules of the common law.

Summary: **Right to jury in civil cases over $20 in value.**

Amendment 8:   Excessive bail shall not be required, nor excessive fines imposed, nor cruel and unusual punishments inflicted.

Summary: **No excessive bail or fines or cruel and unusual punishments.**

Amendment 9:   The enumeration in the Constitution, of certain rights, shall not be construed to deny or disparage others retained by the people.

Summary: **The Constitution shall not deny other rights of people.**

Amendment 10:   The powers not delegated to the United States by the Constitution, nor prohibited by it to the States, are reserved to the States respectively, or to the people.

Summary: **State powers are acknowledged.**

"Why has the government been instituted at all? Because the passions of men will not conform to the dictates of reason and justice without constraint."

Citizens of the United Stastes have the right to assemble peaceably.

Name _____ Date _____

Do You Know Your (Bill of) Rights?

Tell which amendment in the Bill of Rights relates to each of the following examples.
Put the amendment number on the line provided.

_____ 1. A bail of $500 is set for writing bad checks.

_____ 2. The speed limit on state highways is 55 miles per hour (mph).

_____ 3. A gun enthusiast can keep his collection in his/her home.

_____ 4. You can file a lawsuit against the person who ran into your fence with his car.

_____ 5. You can attend the Methodist Church.

_____ 6. During a state of emergency, the National Guard needs shelter for its troops—but not in *my* house!

_____ 7. You are arrested for grand theft auto and your lawyer advises you not to testify at your trial.

_____ 8. You can state your point of view at a town meeting.

_____ 9. You can wear a t-shirt that reads: "Save the Whales!"

_____ 10. States have the right to regulate businesses.

_____ 11. You are arrested and taken directly to court to be tried for your alleged crimes.

_____ 12. You have the right to attend college if you want to.

_____ 13. A policeman, unannounced, walks into your house and begins a search without a search warrant.

_____ 14. You write a letter to the newspaper complaining about the conditions of the city streets.

_____ 15. You petition the school board for longer lunch periods.

Now create five examples of your own!

_____

_____

_____

_____

_____

_____

Name _____ Date _____

Equal or Identical?

Equality means that all people have the same rights and privileges; it does not mean that all people are the same. Equal does not mean identical.

1. Do the same rules about crossing the street apply to preschoolers and high-schoolers alike? Why or why not?

_____

_____

_____

_____

_____

_____

_____

2. Can you think of other instances when the rules for one group of people are different from the rules for another group of people? List as many as you can think of.

_____

_____

_____

_____

_____

_____

_____

_____

_____

Name _____ Date _____

Word Scrambler

Unscramble these "democratic words." Use the word bank at the bottom of the page for clues.

1. WLA _____

2. EDEROFM _____

3. IIBLOGLFRSTH _____

4. EOFNJSEFR _____

5. YLQTEAUI _____

6. TNCSOUTINTIO _____

7. PNTTAREESNRIEO _____

8. OEEVTNGMNR _____

9. AYCMDEORC _____

10. LEDERFA _____

11. EIEEEDNDNCNP _____

12. CDJLAUII _____

13. CITDAAELRNO _____

14. MEALERBP _____

15. EEIILLVASTG _____

Word Bank

Declaration	Law	Legislative
Freedom	Independence	Bill of Rights
Federal	Jefferson	Democracy
Equality	Government	Constitution
Representation	Preamble	Judicial

Name _____ Date _____

Democracy Cryptogram

Decipher these words that relate to democracy (see page 68 for master key).

1. The "boss" of government.

R K R P H G V I R

2. Right to live as you wish.

S E R R Q B Z

3. "That all men are created equal." (three words)

Q R P Y N E N G V B A   B S   V A Q R C R A Q R A P R

4. Every citizen should be treated fairly.

R D H N Y V G L

5. Author of the phrase "life, liberty, and the pursuit of happiness."

W R S S R E F B A

6. It operates at the federal, state, and local levels.

T B I R E A Z R A G

7. Most important document in American history.

P B A F G V G H G V B A

8. A rule or order passed by legislatures.

Y N J

9. The court is called the _____ branch.

W H   Q V P V N Y

10. Something we are allowed to do, such as vote.

E V T U G

Name _____ Date _____

Democracy Word Search Puzzle

Find the words listed below and circle them in the word search puzzle. Words may be printed in the puzzle forward, backward, horizontally, vertically, or diagonally.

```
N S R E W O P F O N O I T A R A P E S P
O N J M O K X F A R A V Q M J I T K S B
B Z E B L H L R P A O B M A T L A W T Q
K A F L O S D E V M F N B J B Y U F H C
N W F Z B Z V E L E N O I O E P O Q G O
O Q E K G J H D Y N L I L R K E N U I M
I E R G A A A O C D F T L I I D Y J R U
T Y S T C Q G M A M F A O T G L E E E U
A J O W Z N H I R E V R F Y O I V L L L
T N N H J K V L C N R A R R V B I B B E
N F E D E R A L O T A L I U E E T M A V
E T A T S Q U N M S C C G L R R U A N I
S N A C M R L N E M X E H E N T C E E T
E V H J P Y K P D Y G D T D M Y E R I A
R C G I M M I G R A N T S W E W X P L L
P Y N O I T U T I T S N O C N X E O A S
E L A I C I D U J C L S S S T R H V N I
R S S E L C I T R A Y T I L A U Q E U G
D X D K V A V Y I N D E P E N D E N C E
M P M W B U Z R L O C A L F J R L S T L
```

WORD LIST

amendments	articles	Bill of Rights	Constitution
declaration	democracy	equality	executive
federal	freedom	government	immigrants
independence	Jefferson	judicial	law
legislative	liberty	local	majority rule
preamble	representation	separation of powers	
state	unalienable rights		

Name _____ Date _____

Democracy Crossword Puzzle

Use the clues below to complete the crossword puzzle.

ACROSS

1. Citizens participate in government by _____ or running for office.
4. The right to live as we choose
8. The right to participate in government
12. Chief executive of a state
13. First ten amendments to the Constitution (three words)
14. Congress is the _____ branch of government.
15. Citizens treated fairly

DOWN

2. Operates at federal, state, and local levels
3. Another word for the right to vote
5. Author of the Declaration of Independence
6. Basic principle of the U.S. government
7. Chief executive of the United States
9. Symbol of democracy in New York Harbor (three words)
10. In a democracy, the _____ rules.
11. Most important document of the U.S. government

Law

A *law* is a statement or rule that tells us what we may or may not do. There is a federal law, for example, that prevents anyone besides the federal government from printing or minting money. In order for a law to be "legal" or valid it must have a clear definition and a penalty. There are two broad sets of laws known as criminal and civil laws.

All laws must follow the broad limits of the United States Constitution. The purpose of any law is to help regulate a nation (federal), geographic area (state), or city (local). Laws create order out of chaos. Without laws citizens would be unable to enjoy the benefits of their freedom.

Our nation is governed by the principles of *rule of law* and *due process*. Rule of law refers to the idea that all people must obey the law; no one is considered above or outside the law. Due process means that all citizens should be treated equally and fairly when a law is applied to them. A democratic society requires that both principles be enforced in order to promote justice. It would not be possible to live without these principles in our structure of government.

Imagine that you and your friends were washed ashore on a tropical island. The island is uninhabited but has ample food, water, and shelter for everyone. No one owns the island, and no one knows you are there. You may be trapped on the island for days or years. Would you want to have laws to help the group live together peacefully? If so, describe some of these laws. If not, how do you know that everyone would behave correctly? William Golding wrote about how a party of young people survived in this setting in his book, *Lord of the Flies.* You may want to read this book to get a better idea of how laws affect a community. Jot down a few ideas that you think would enable your group to live together in peace in a situation such as the one mentioned above.

Yeah, I would have some laws. One law I would have is no killing anyone. Another law I would have is no stealing

"No man is above the law and no man is below it; nor do we ask any man's mission when we require him to obey it. Obedience to the law is demanded as a right; not asked as a favor."

-Theodore Roosevelt-

Name _____ Date _____

Fair vs. Unfair Laws

Based on our discussion of democracy and the law, decide whether the following laws would be fair or unfair. Rate them according to your opinion as to what is a "good" versus a "bad" law. Have an explanation in mind for each answer.

_____ Males at age eighteen must register for military services.

_____ All businesses need a license to operate.

_____ People are allowed to keep poisonous pets at home.

_____ Guns may not be fired within city limits.

_____ Left-handed children must sit in the back of their classrooms in school.

_____ Dogs must be walked on a leash.

_____ There must be height and weight requirements for airplane pilots.

_____ Religious materials may not be handed out in public parks.

_____ People may not picket outside a doctor's office.

_____ Wage earners need to pay federal and state income tax.

_____ People with AIDS should not be allowed to work in hospitals.

_____ People who own three or more pets may not apply for welfare benefits.

_____ Senior citizens are entitled to a 10% discount for any type of purchase.

_____ All mentally ill citizens must be placed in hospital care.

List some examples of other laws that you consider to be "fair" (good) or "unfair" (bad).

1. _____

2. _____

3. _____

4. _____

5. _____

6. _____

United States Government

The government of the United States is organized at three levels: federal, state, and local. Each level of government contains three branches, known as the *executive, legislative,* and *judicial.* These branches (or arms) of government perform certain duties and functions for its citizens. This arrangement of duties between the three levels is called *the structure of government* or *separation of powers.* Generally, the legislative branch is responsible for making laws, the judicial branch for interpreting the laws, and the executive branch for enforcing the laws.

A simple way to keep the levels and branches straight is by reviewing the chart below. Think of it as a "who's who and what's what" guide to government.

Division of Government Powers			
	Executive	**Legislative**	**Judicial**
Federal	President	Congress	Federal Courts
State	Governor	State Assembly	State Courts
Local	Mayor	City Council/ Board of Aldermen	Municipal Courts

The federal government takes priority over the other two levels (state and local) because it deals with issues that may affect all citizens. The powers of the federal government include taxation, declaring war upon another nation, passing laws, and regulating commerce. State and local governments are allowed to pass laws on matters that pertain just to their state or city.

Our national (federal) system of government is empowered to govern us because of the U.S. Constitution, which is supported by federal laws, court decisions, and administrative rules. The will of the people is expressed in the Constitution, which created a strong central government. It is so strong, in fact, that the sole power reserved exclusively for states is the right to exist. Only a state, in other words, may decide to exist or not. In all other matters and issues, the federal government is sovereign, or supreme, in its authority to rule over its citizens.

3

Name _____ Date _____

Declaration of Independence

"We hold these truths to be self-evident: That all men are created equal; that they are endowed by their Creator with certain unalienable rights; that among these are life, liberty and the pursuit of happiness; that, to secure these rights, governments are instituted among men, deriving their just powers from the consent of the governed; that whenever any form of government becomes destructive of these ends, it is the right of the people to alter or abolish it. . . ."

Thomas Jefferson authored the Declaration of Independence. The Second Continental Congress adopted the Declaration on July 4, 1776. It reflects the basic principles of our nation.

Which of the three principles of democracy (freedom, equality, representation), in your opinion, best matches these statements from the Declaration of Independence? Why do you believe they match?

Freedom—Equality—Representation

1. _____ "All men are created equal"

Reason: _____

2. _____ "Unalienable rights"

Reason: _____

3. _____ "Life, liberty, and the pursuit of happiness"

Reason: _____

4. _____ "Consent of the governed"

Reason: _____

Thomas Jefferson could not have foreseen the needs and expectations of today's multicultural nation, which is so much different from the nation of early American settlers that he knew. Think of some ways that people pursue happiness today without hurting or interfering with others.

Name _____ Date _____

Civil Law

There are two general types of law—civil and criminal. *Civil law* deals with the personal and property rights of people, such as signing a contract to buy a house, getting married or divorced, and paying taxes. A dispute over one or more of these rights is resolved in a civil court through a *lawsuit.* The person who decides to sue someone is called a *plaintiff.* If a plaintiff sues and wins a lawsuit, he or she may be given an award (money) to be paid by the *defendant,* or loser of the lawsuit. The plaintiff could be one person or a group (such as a business or governing body). The defendant could also be an organization.

"The Case of the Lost Vacation"

Milo Manheim is a carpenter who saved $3,000 in order to spend two weeks of vacation in Hawaii. He booked all of his travel arrangements with EZ-GO Lucky, a local discount travel agency. The package deal cost $3,000 and included the airfare, hotel, meals—everything! Milo had waited two years to save up enough money to go on his dream vacation.

Ten days before his departure Milo went to the travel agency to pick up his airplane tickets. The large sign outside the agency read "Out of Business." Greatly upset, Milo hurried to his attorney and had him file a lawsuit against EZ-GO Lucky. "Sue those crooks!" he yelled to the lawyer. "I want my $3,000 back!"

Milo the plaintiff had his day in court. The judge listened to his complaint and to the responses of EZ-GO Lucky's attorney. In the end, Milo was awarded $3,000 by the judge. Even though Milo didn't make it to Hawaii, he did manage to get his money refunded.

Do you feel that Milo received "justice"? Explain your answer.

_____

_____

_____

_____

_____

_____

_____

_____

Name _____ Date _____

Everyday Laws

Civil laws are made at all three levels of government. They affect virtually all of us during our lifetimes. The following is a list of topics covered by civil laws in the United States. Place a check mark next to the issues that have affected you or relate to your life.

_____ birth certificate   _____ driver's license

_____ getting a polio shot   _____ walking your dog on a leash

_____ storing toxic waste in containers   _____ wearing clothes in public

_____ having a social security number   _____ applying for a credit card

_____ getting a prescription drug   _____ no parking near fire hydrants

_____ building codes   _____ regulation of waterways

_____ food sales to customers   _____ auto inspections

_____ emergency hospital care   _____ paying taxes

_____ movie ratings   _____ going to school

_____ flying an airplane   _____ enlisting in the military

Can you think of any other civil laws that affect you?

_____

_____

_____

_____

_____

_____

_____

_____

_____

Criminal Law

Criminal law centers on acts that offend some-one, their property, or society. Such acts are called crimes or offenses and are ranked according to their severity. A *felony* is the most serious category of crime. Arson, murder, robbery, and treason are a few ex-amples of felonies. A *misdemeanor* is viewed as a lesser type of crime. The outcome of a misdemeanor is not as severe as the outcome of a felony. Forging someone's name on a check and petty theft are misdemeanors, and are less important than felonies like arson or treason. A violation of an *ordinance* is a minor offense done within a community. Bans on littering and dogs without leashes in public are com-mon types of ordinances. The penalty for committing a crime varies according to the type and severity of the crime. A cold-blooded murder may, in some states, qualify for *capital punishment* (the death penalty). Bicycle theft, on the other hand, is a minor crime that would probably result in a fine imposed by the courts.

How can we tell the difference between a criminal wrong and a civil wrong? A crime is a public wrong directed at society. Robbing a bank is a public wrong. The government has an interest in preventing and prosecuting crimes because of its responsibility to protect society. A bank robber acts against the best interests of government and also threatens society's safety. If he is not caught and punished, he may continue to endanger a variety of people. Someone accused of a crime and brought to trial is called a defendant.

A civil wrong, however, offends a person's rights or possessions but does not involve the government directly or as a party. If you sue someone because he or she refuses to pay back a debt, then you are saying a civil wrong has occurred.

For a criminal law to be valid it must include two features: (1) a clear definition of a crime, and (2) a reasonable punishment. The definition will describe what we must or must not do to or for each other. Some laws require us to do something; failing to do so is called a *crime of omission* (for instance, failing to obtain a driver's license before beginning to drive). A *crime of commission* is one in which we do something that the law says we mustn't do, such as driving over the speed limit.

Criminal laws serve many purposes. They deter people from crimes of commission or omission. They punish offenders and reform some of those found guilty of crimes. Criminal laws also offer society a degree of safety and protection from people who refuse or are unable to live within the law.

"We must not make a scarecrow of the law, Setting it up to fear the birds of prey, And let it keep one shape, till custom make it Their perch, and not their terror."

-William Shakespeare-

Name _____ Date _____

Just Desserts or Injustice?

Miss Laura Petite stole $1,000,000 from a local bank. She was caught and prosecuted, but the jury did not find her guilty of the charge. Two years later, Laura was once again arrested for robbery. This time, however, she did not commit the crime. In court the jury found her guilty. The judge gave Miss Petite a sentence of 15 years in prison (for something she did not do).

Do you think justice was served in this case? Why or why not?

_____

_____

_____

_____

_____

_____

_____

_____

_____

"My object all sublime
I shall achieve in time—
To make the punishment fit the crime."

-W.S. Gilbert-

Name _____ Date _____

Criminal or Civil Wrong?

Take a look at the following examples. Try to decide if a crime or a civil wrong has occurred. Write either "crime," "civil," or "both" beside each example. Be prepared to explain your choices.

_____ 1. Someone refuses to pay their city water bill.

_____ 2. A driver refuses to take a breathalyzer test.

_____ 3. A neighbor accidentally mows over your prize petunias.

_____ 4. There are loud, all night parties at the house next door.

_____ 5. Someone writes a check for groceries knowing there is no money left in the bank account.

_____ 6. Someone intentionally puts less money in a parking meter than is required.

_____ 7. Someone refuses to help a law enforcement officer when ordered to do so.

_____ 8. Someone makes a $2 wager on the outcome of a professional football game.

_____ 9. There are cockroaches and rats in the kitchen of a popular restaurant.

_____ 10. A company uses false advertising.

_____ 11. Someone is caught fishing without a license.

_____ 12. A person borrows a neighbor's car without permission.

_____ 13. A factory dumps toxic waste into the water supply.

_____ 14. The train engineer is found to be operating a train while he is intoxicated.

_____ 15. A pickpocket puts his hand in the empty pocket of a stranger.

_____ 16. A car manufacturer knowingly makes defective autos.

_____ 17. Someone forgets to put their seatbelt on in the front seat of a car.

_____ 18. A hospital overcharges for its services.

_____ 19. Someone takes a shopping cart home.

_____ 20. A surgeon operates, but removes the wrong organ from the patient.

Name _____ Date _____

What Am I?

Definitions are provided for words that were covered in this section. On the line following each definition, write the word described.

1. A statement about what we may or may not do. _____

2. When a law requires us to do something and we don't do it. _____

3. Person who sues another in civil court. _____

4. Laws that refer to crimes. _____

5. A major or serious crime. _____

6. Person accused of a crime. _____

7. A law that is enacted by communities about a less serious offense. _____

8. Money "won" in civil court. _____

9. No one is above or outside the law. _____

10. Laws that relate to civil issues like marriage. _____

11. Branch of government that makes laws. _____

12. Author of the Declaration of Independence. _____

13. Contains preamble, seven articles, and 27 amendments. _____

14. Three parts of criminal justice system. _____

15. First ten amendments to the Constitution. _____

16. People responsible for enforcing the laws. _____

17. An example of a sentence (punishment). _____

18. Three basic principles of a democracy. _____

19. A criminal law includes a definition and a _____

20. One purpose of criminal law. _____

Name _____ Date _____

That's Not Fair!

1. Sometimes laws are made that may not be fair, or just, to everyone who is affected by the law. Is breaking an unjust law an effective strategy to bring about change? (Think about the implications of breaking ANY law.) Why or why not? If not, what would be an effective method to change an unjust law?

_____

_____

_____

_____

_____

_____

_____

_____

2. What laws (civil or criminal), if any, would you like to see changed? Why?

_____

_____

_____

_____

_____

_____

_____

_____

Name _____ Date _____

Law Word Scrambler

Unscramble these words that relate to law. Use the word bank if you need to.

1. EDUOSESRPC _____

2. WLALINCMRAI _____

3. AWLFOMISSOION _____

4. ELRUFOWAL _____

5. OFYELN _____

6. SOCRUT _____

7. VIILCALW _____

8. TFEANNDDE _____

9. WAADR _____

10. NNOEDCRIA _____

11. FLAITFPIN _____

12. ROMEANSIMED _____

13. RSRIUOCTTLA _____

14. BYERORB _____

15. AWLFOOMOMSISICN _____

Word Bank

ordinance	due process	award
criminal law	robbery	defendant
law of omission	civil law	plaintiff
rule of law	federal	felony
law of commission	misdemeanor	state
courts	penalty	reasonable
trial courts	local	

Name _____ Date _____

Law Cryptogram

Decipher these words that relate to law (see page 68 for master key).

1. Laws that deal with crimes (two words)

$$\overline{P}\,\overline{E}\,\overline{V}\,\overline{Z}\quad\overline{V}\,\overline{A}\,\overline{N}\,\overline{Y}\qquad\overline{Y}\,\overline{N}\,\overline{J}\,\overline{F}$$

2. A major or serious crime is called a _____ .

$$\overline{S}\,\overline{R}\,\overline{Y}\,\overline{B}\,\overline{A}\,\overline{L}$$

3. A crime is a public wrong directed at _____ .

$$\overline{F}\,\overline{B}\,\overline{P}\,\overline{V}\,\overline{R}\,\overline{G}\,\overline{L}$$

4. First ten amendments of the U.S. Constitution (three words)

$$\overline{O}\,\overline{V}\,\overline{Y}\,\overline{Y}\quad\overline{B}\,\overline{S}\quad\overline{E}\,\overline{V}\,\overline{T}\,\overline{U}\,\overline{G}\,\overline{F}$$

5. A minor or lesser crime is called a _____ .

$$\overline{Z}\,\overline{V}\,\overline{F}\,\overline{Q}\,\overline{R}\,\overline{Z}\,\overline{R}\,\overline{N}\,\overline{A}\,\overline{B}\,\overline{E}$$

6. There are federal, _____ , and local laws.

$$\overline{F}\,\overline{G}\,\overline{N}\,\overline{G}\,\overline{R}$$

7. Laws that refer to civil issues such as marriage (two words)

$$\overline{P}\,\overline{V}\,\overline{I}\,\overline{V}\,\overline{Y}\qquad\overline{Y}\,\overline{N}\,\overline{J}\,\overline{F}$$

8. Person accused of a crime

$$\overline{Q}\,\overline{R}\,\overline{S}\,\overline{R}\,\overline{A}\,\overline{Q}\,\overline{N}\,\overline{A}\,\overline{G}$$

9. Idea that no one is above the law (three words)

$$\overline{E}\,\overline{H}\,\overline{Y}\,\overline{R}\quad\overline{B}\,\overline{S}\quad\overline{Y}\,\overline{N}\,\overline{J}$$

10. All citizens treated fairly when a law is applied to them (two words)

$$\overline{Q}\,\overline{H}\,\overline{R}\quad\overline{C}\,\overline{E}\,\overline{B}\,\overline{P}\,\overline{R}\,\overline{F}\,\overline{F}$$

Name _____   Date _____

Law Word Search Puzzle

Find the words listed below and circle them in the word search puzzle. Words may be printed in the puzzle forward, backward, horizontally, vertically, or diagonally.

```
R Q C R I M E O F O M I S S I O N B D T
M O M I K C I V I L L A W B H U Y O H N
O V M I C S S E C O R P E U D G G Y E
C R J X R E A S O N A B L E A N L G P M
W T N E M H S I N U P L A T I P A C B N
D K F L M I S D E M E A N O R B Q T E R
R N O I S S I M M O C F O E M I R C S E
A B T B E P U N I S H M E N T O D S J V
W A C L E A R D E F I N I T I O N J L O
A L E L W L W A L F O E L U R K Z M X G
A P A R Y A V E F N E O R D I N A N C E
M X E W P L A I N T I F F L F M K K T Y
X J F N S S L O A Y Z E Y Q A E A S P Y
L S U W A U M O V T N T K A S R L A V Q
K T X D W L I I C P R Z C K G I E O B J
L A U W G F T T Y A T R U O C G A D N Y
D T Q L L E Y Y J D L W O E H O S I E Y
J E G X E T F H S S J M P K F C M B L F
D E C I T S U J U T N A D N E F E D P Q
M W A L L A N I M I R C E M K K Y S P N
```

WORD LIST

award	capital punishment	civil law
clear definition	court	crime of commission
crime of omission	criminal law	defendant
due process	federal	felony
government	judge	justice
lawsuit	local	misdemeanor
ordinance	penalty	plaintiff
punishment	reasonable	rule of law
state		

Name _____ Date _____

Law Crossword Puzzle

Use the clues below to complete the crossword puzzle.

ACROSS

1. A lesser crime
6. A major crime
9. The boss of the court
10. Money to be paid by the loser of a lawsuit
12. Law relating to civil acts (two words)
14. When we don't do something the law says we should (three words)
15. Law pertaining to crimes (two words)

DOWN

2. Person accused of a crime
3. No one is outside or beyond the law (three words).
4. Person who files a lawsuit
5. A violation of an _____ is a minor offense.
7. Statement telling us what we may or may not do
8. The death penalty (two words)
11. When we do something the law says we mustn't (three words)
13. Disputes are resolved in civil court through ____.

The System of Justice

Our system of justice is organized at the federal, state, and local levels of government. There are, in fact, two separate criminal justice systems, one for adults and the other for juveniles (minors). Each of these systems has three similar parts known as the *police, courts,* and *corrections.*

The police are responsible for enforcing the laws. Different types of police agencies enforce different laws and regulations. Federal park rangers, for instance, help keep order at national recreation areas like Yellowstone National Park.

The courts administer justice by hearing cases. We have a *dual court system* in America. This means two systems—a federal and a state system—exist side by side. Federal courts are only allowed to try cases involving federal crimes. State courts preside over the crimes of their respective states. Regardless of whether the system is federal or state, we can identify two basic types of courts. Trial courts hear cases and decide guilt or innocence. Appeals (appellate) courts review the procedures and penalties of the trial courts to see if they were lawful and just.

Corrections deals with the punishments of people who are convicted of crimes. The punishment is known as a *sentence* and may consist of one or more of the following items: imprisonment (prison or jail), probation, parole, fines, community work service, house arrest, restitution, and electronic monitoring.

The goal of corrections is to deter people from criminal acts. Moreover, sentences are used to help rehabilitate or improve offenders. We, as a society, are entitled to punish criminals who have hurt us or our property. To rehabilitate an offender means that he has "changed his ways" and is willing to lead a lawful life upon release. Not all offenders, however, are able or willing to change; for them, incarceration in a jail or prison is a way of life and necessary for the safety of communities. No one, after all, wants to be the victim of a crime. Locking up certain offenders reduces the risk of victimization.

The criminal justice system (adult and juvenile) is huge, complex, and widespread. Its purposes are to enforce the law (police), hear cases (courts), and punish the guilty (corrections). In so doing, the system of justice makes it possible for us to live in and enjoy the benefits of a relatively safe society.

"I think the first duty of society is justice."

-Alexander Hamilton-

Judicial Process: Steps and Procedures

Due process requires that equal treatment is to be given to each person accused of a crime. Each defendant will, with some exceptions, be processed by the courts in roughly the same way.

Let us take a brief look at the basic steps and procedures of a typical case:

STEP 1:   *Investigation* by the police of a reported crime.

STEP 2:   *Arrest* of a *suspect* (someone believed to be the offender).

STEP 3:   *Booking:* the suspect is detained at a jail, fingerprinted, photographed, and told of the charges against him.

STEP 4:   *Initial appearance:* the defendant (accused person) makes his first court appearance. He is told of his rights, the charges are read aloud, and bail is decided. Some of the defendant's rights include the right to an attorney, the right to reasonable bail, and the right to remain silent.

STEP 5:   *Information* or *indictment:* documents issued by a prosecutor (information) or grand jury (indictment) that list all of the charges against a suspect. Less than half of the states require the use of a grand jury trial to determine whether or not the government should prosecute an accused person. Some states rely on the preliminary hearing. This means a judge reviews the evidence to see if there is enough evidence (a valid case) to continue toward a trial.

STEP 6:   *Arraignment:* defendant pleads "guilty" or "not guilty" to the charges. Charges may be dismissed at this point.

STEP 7:   *Trial* or *guilty plea:* Someone who tries to get the sentence, number of crimes, or types of crimes reduced or changed in exchange for a guilty plea is plea bargaining. Almost 90 percent of all criminal cases are resolved in this way. Very few persons accused of a felony ever seek a trial to determine guilt or innocence.

STEP 8:   *Sentencing.*

STEP 9:   *Corrections:* For civil cases, a typical penalty is a fine. Failure to pay a fine may result in a jail sentence or probation. For criminal cases, a convicted person may be imprisoned, fined, or given an alternative sentence.

STEP 10:   *Appeal:* Our system of justice permits a convicted person to appeal his or her conviction to a court of appeal. Like trials, only a few criminal defendants are successful with their appeals. Most verdicts are upheld by appellate courts.

Courtroom Actors

Virtually every criminal court in the United States has a group of officials (actors) who manage the daily business of the court. These actors work together every day, and each performs a variety of tasks. The many types of cases brought before the courts are successfully processed due to their efforts. Some of these actors and their duties will be familiar to you.

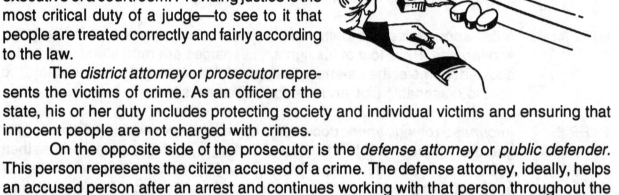

To begin with, the *judge* is the chief executive of a courtroom. Providing justice is the most critical duty of a judge—to see to it that people are treated correctly and fairly according to the law.

The *district attorney* or *prosecutor* represents the victims of crime. As an officer of the state, his or her duty includes protecting society and individual victims and ensuring that innocent people are not charged with crimes.

On the opposite side of the prosecutor is the *defense attorney* or *public defender*. This person represents the citizen accused of a crime. The defense attorney, ideally, helps an accused person after an arrest and continues working with that person throughout the trial process.

The *bailiff,* typically a police officer, has many duties that help the court function correctly. Among other responsibilities, a bailiff keeps order in the court, supervises the jury, and protects the judge.

A *court reporter* or *recorder* keeps an accurate record of what happens during the course of a trial. This is done through the use of an audio tape recorder or a stenotype machine. The finished product is known as an official record of a trial and is often put into the form of a document.

The *clerk of the court* is an administrator who aids the judge in running the court. Record keeper and "paper pusher," the clerk performs many behind-the-scenes duties, such as preparing a jury list, that keep the court operating efficiently.

There are two types of *witnesses*—expert and lay. An expert witness will testify about an area in which he or she has a specialized skill. Fingerprinting, handwriting analysis, and blood testing are examples of scientific evidence. A lay witness is also known as a character or eyewitness and is permitted to speak about non-scientific issues in court.

Lastly, no case may exist without a *defendant* and a *victim.* They are the reason for having all of the other actors present in court. The victim is the person who is pursuing the lawsuit. The defendant is the person accused of committing the crime. Together, each person fulfills a necessary role in the pursuit of justice.

Court

Courts can be found at the federal, state, and local levels. A court is both a real and a symbolic agency of government. As a real agency, courts are rectangular shaped rooms where judicial actors—judges, prosecutors, and others—gather to administer the law and dole out justice. Symbolically, courts stand for the principle that "justice is blind"; all citizens who enter a court, in other words, should be treated fairly, whether the case is serious or minor in nature. For this reason, courts of justice are expected to fulfill five essential duties.

Court Functions

1. Serve as a symbol of justice
2. Settle disputes
3. Protect society from crime
4. Punish offenders
5. Provide a natural setting for "doing" justice

A dispute brought before a court is referred to as a *case*, a *lawsuit*, or a *complaint*. A court must first figure out the facts of a case and then determine what laws apply to it. In a civil case the defendant may be ordered to pay a flat sum of money to the plaintiff. Criminal courts, however, have the authority to impose extra penalties besides a fine, such as a prison sentence or community work service.

The judge is the chief executive of a court. He or she is responsible for seeing to it that a court runs efficiently. Courts have no power to enforce their decisions. They must depend on other agencies, like the police or probation officers, to make certain that their rulings are upheld. A convicted felon, for instance, placed on house arrest by the court, will be supervised by a probation officer. However, courts have at their disposal the full power of the state to impose penalties upon the defendants.

"The judge should not be young; he should have learned to know evil, not from his own soul, but from late and long observation of the nature of evil in others; knowledge should be his guide, not personal experience."

-Plato-

Name _____ Date _____

Who's Who in Court?

Match the job description in column A with the job title in column B.

_____ 1. Chief of the court   A. Bailiff

_____ 2. Accused person   B. Defendant

_____ 3. Eyewitness   C. Prosecutor

_____ 4. Scientific witness   D. Defense attorney

_____ 5. Protects judge and jury   E. Clerk of the court

_____ 6. Represents the state's case   F. Court reporter

_____ 7. Gives the accused legal guidance   G. Expert witness

_____ 8. Handles paperwork of the court   H. Lay witness

_____ 9. Keeps record of trial   I. Judge

_____ 10. Person claiming a wrong was done to him/her   J. Victim

What's What in Court

Match the court term in column A with the definition in column B.

_____ 1. Stenotype machine   A. All citizens are to be treated fairly in courts of law.

_____ 2. Complaint   B. Dispute brought before a court.

_____ 3. Penalties   C. Dispute between two people.

_____ 4. "Justice is blind"   D. Facts that may prove innocence or guilt.

_____ 5. Jury   E. Administration of law in a fair way.

_____ 6. Evidence   F. Keeps accurate record of what's happening in court.

_____ 7. Court   G. Prosecution is the state.

_____ 8. Civil case   H. What must be done or paid when defendant is guilty.

_____ 9. Criminal case   I. Group of peers called in to decide guilt or innocence.

_____ 10. Justice   J. Where a trial is held.

Judge

The judge is the key officer of the court. The principal job of a judge is to administer the law. This means that he or she is the chief officer of a court and must preside over all civil or criminal cases brought before the court. A judge is essentially the "boss" of the courtroom; everyone within it must obey the judge's orders.

If someone misbehaves or fails to follow a judge's instructions, that person may be cited with *contempt of court*. In other words, a judge may order a person to be fined or placed in jail for misconduct. For instance, a defendant accused of auto theft who starts yelling at the witnesses may be charged with contempt of court.

A judge's powers and responsibilities are impressive. But how does a person become a judge? There are four methods for selecting a judge. The first is through a popular election; citizens use the ballot box to vote for their favorite candidate. The candidate who receives the most votes "wins" the position of judge.

A second method is by appointment. Governors and the President of the United States can, in certain cases, appoint someone to be a state or federal judge. A governor may use executive authority to appoint someone to the position of state judge in the event of a vacancy. The president must nominate a candidate who is then reviewed by the U.S. Senate for qualifications and ability. Assuming that the Senate agrees with the president, the candidate is approved to serve as a federal judge.

The third approach is to select a judge on the basis of merit or qualifications. Once chosen, the new judge must periodically run for the office through popular election.

The fourth method, in which the state legislature decides who will be a judge, is used in three states. The legislature reviews eligible candidates and makes its decision.

Once elected or appointed, a judge must begin the job of running a courtroom. These duties include the following:

• Administering daily courtroom activities
• Hearing cases and conducting trials
• Issuing instructions to juries
• Handing out decisions on motions and cases
• Protecting the rights of the accused
• Pronouncing penalties or punishments for people convicted in civil or criminal cases
• Resolving plea bargains

Name _____ Date _____

Judge (cont.)

An efficient, effective judge will keep the court *docket* up-to-date. A docket is the calendar which lists all of the cases scheduled to be heard by a judge. A percentage of criminal cases will be resolved by a *plea bargain* instead of proceeding to a trial. In a plea bargain, a defendant agrees to plead guilty in return for some concessions from the court. These concessions may consist of a reduced sentence or reduced charges.

From a judge's point of view, a speedy trial or a plea bargain will help move cases along the docket. Balancing the necessity to move cases on the docket with society's need for justice is a difficult task. Being a good judge, therefore, requires legal experience, wisdom, and common sense.

"Judgment is not the knowledge of fundamental laws; it is knowing how to apply a knowledge of them."

-Charles Gow-

Using the quote above as a guide, explain what sort of qualifications a judge should have in order to perform the duties of his job. Also, describe what type of person in your opinion would make a "bad" judge. Why do you feel this way?

_____
_____
_____
_____
_____
_____
_____
_____
_____
_____
_____

Name _____ Date _____

My Place or Yours?

Imagine yourself as one of the nine judges of the U.S. Supreme Court, the highest court in the nation. It is your first day on the job. The case presented to the judges seems simple enough in its facts.

J.R. O'Reilly owns a house in the hills of northern California. Eight months ago, during a mud slide, O'Reilly's house tumbled down the hill and landed in the backyard of Jamal Chatham. Mr. Chatham declared that O'Reilly's house was now his property due to its location. O'Reilly claims a freak accident of nature—the mud slide—moved his home and he still retains ownership.

Who is right? How would you decide this case? Briefly defend your position.

_____

_____

_____

_____

_____

_____

_____

_____

_____

_____

_____

_____

Criminal Trial

A *trial* is a process by which the facts and issues surrounding a case are reviewed and decided upon in court. The outcome of this process is a *verdict* or *judgment.* A typical criminal case, however, does not usually proceed to trial, but is resolved through a *guilty plea.* Those cases that do go to trial will be heard and judged either by a judge (bench trial) or a jury (jury trial).

Most citizens will never view or go through an actual trial process. Unfortunately, the popular media, such as films and television shows, gives us a distorted view of trials. In these make-believe settings, the trial resembles a drama where the "good guys" triumph in the end. Occasionally, courtroom actors in the media are allowed to behave in ways that are clearly illegal or false. For example, in real life, a defense attorney may not bring in a "surprise" witness at the end of a trial.

In a jury trial, the jurors must decide if the accused is guilty or not guilty.

In a trial the truth is found and tested. Questions are answered about the "who, what, when, where, and why" of a case. Hopefully by the end of this search for answers, a just and fair verdict will be reached. In order to get to that point it is first necessary to complete all of the stages involved in the trial process. Let's assume in the following case that a jury trial is about to begin.

One Dumb Robber

A 19-year-old student, Jake Merriweather, was charged with the crime of first degree armed robbery. On September 14, 1995, Jake walked into a crowded coffee shop and pulled out a large pistol. He demanded money from the customers and cashier. Putting the loot in a brown bag, Jake fled to the get-away car parked outside the shop. As he tried to drive away, his car stalled. He then jumped out and hailed a taxi.

Jake had dropped his wallet with a driver's license in the coffee shop. He forgot the bag of money in the stalled car in his hurry to flee the scene of the crime. The police found the car, his wallet, the stolen money, and minutes later, Jake, who was emptying water from his fake pistol. Jake was promptly arrested and booked. The court appointed a lawyer to represent him and Jake entered a plea of not guilty to the charges read to him. Bail was set at $1,000 but Jake, lacking money, had to sit in jail and await his trial date. The case of *The State v. Jake Merriweather* has begun!

The State v. Jake Merriweather

STEP ONE is the *opening statement*. The prosecutor (state) goes first, followed by the defense attorney. Both sides will explain to the jury briefly what they wish to prove and how that will be done. Offering *evidence* is one way to help prove something in court. Evidence consists of facts and information about a case such as witnesses or physical evidence (fake pistol).

STEP TWO involves the *presentation of the state's case*. The burden of proving an accused person (defendant) committed a crime is always on the state. A defendant is assumed to be innocent until proven guilty. The prosecutor will provide all of the state's evidence to the jury for it to evaluate.

STEP THREE is identical to step two except this time it is the *presentation of the*

The verdict is read aloud in court.

defense's case. The defense attorney for the accused person has an opportunity to show why his or her client is either innocent or justified in committing the crime. Like a prosecutor, the defense attorney may present evidence to the jury.

STEP FOUR, which is called *closing arguments,* begins once both sides are finished presenting their cases. The prosecutor and defense attorney give their final statements to the jury. These remarks focus on the strengths (prosecutor) or weaknesses (defense) of the state's case.

STEP FIVE centers on the *jury deliberations* or review of the case. Members of the jury are placed in a private conference room and ordered to reach a *verdict,* if they can, by the judge. A verdict is the final decision, or judgment, of a jury. It is arrived at after a careful discussion of the facts of a case followed by a vote as to whether the accused person is guilty or not guilty.

STEP SIX is *reading the verdict aloud* in court. A "not guilty" verdict means the trial is over and the defendant is free to go. A "guilty" verdict, however, leads to a final step.

In STEP SEVEN *sentencing* occurs. A guilty defendant may be fined, put in prison, placed on probation, or given a mix of different penalties allowed by law. The sentence will depend, naturally, on the seriousness of the crime.

P.S. Jake Merriweather received a suspended sentence and was forbidden to drive. He was also forbidden to own real or fake weapons.

Name _____ Date _____

Salem Witch Trials

Much has been written about the famous witch hunts and trials of Salem, Massachusetts, that occurred in 1692. The belief in witchcraft remained popular in colonial America. Demons, devils, warlocks, and evil spirits were thought to be active, dangerous agents of the supernatural.

The Salem witch trials lasted from March to September of 1692. They began when two young girls were labeled as bewitched. A mass hysteria soon resulted. People began reporting visions and incidents that featured women involved in spellcasting, shape-changing, and animal behavior. None of the reports or "sightings" had any evidence to support them. It was enough to simply state one's belief in the satanic powers of another person. That "other person"—almost always a woman—was then hauled before a special seven-member court.

Many of the normal rules of evidence were ignored. The court was ordered by Governor Phips to try all prisoners accused of dealing in witchery. The defendants were not allowed to have a lawyer to help them. In the end, 27 people were found guilty; 19 of them were hanged. Giles Corey, one of the few male defendants, was pressed to death by rocks. Hundreds of others confessed or were imprisoned.

Finally, Governor Phips stepped in. He ordered the release of all prisoners and suspects. Evidence against every accused witch was found to be made up and aimed at unpopular women in Salem. The hunt for witches was over.

Why were women (rather than men) most often labeled and prosecuted as witches?

_____

_____

_____

_____

_____

_____

_____

Name _____ Date _____

A Court of Errors

Read through the following case. Spot the mistakes related to courts and trials. Briefly write down the mistakes at the end of the case. There are 11 mistakes to find.

"Your Honor!" the prosecutor said in protest. "My client is accused of arson. The building never burned down. How can he be charged with setting fire to it?"

"Easy," replied the clerk of court. "He had a can of gasoline and matches in his hand when the police arrived."

The prosecutor frowned and sat down. His client wanted to enter a verdict before the trial began. Things were not going well. The bailiff's docket was broken. The judge had filed a complaint with the victim. Even the clerk of court refused to be helpful.

After closing statements, both sides—the state and the defense—presented their cases. No evidence was allowed. Not even the gas can and matches. The defense attorney was ordered to also serve as a juror.

"This trial is too stupid!" yelled the prosecutor. "Judges aren't supposed to say anything during a trial. I've had enough! I am going to let the court reporter represent my client." Which he did and exited the courtroom.

In the end, his ex-client was found "sort of, somewhat, almost, not quite guilty" by the jury!

Errors

1. _____

2. _____

3. _____

4. _____

5. _____

6. _____

7. _____

8. _____

9. _____

10. _____

11. _____

Name _____ Date _____

Court Cryptogram

Decipher these words that relate to courts (see page 68 for master key).

1. Person accused of a crime

$$\overline{Q}\ \overline{R}\ \overline{S}\ \overline{R}\ \overline{A}\ \overline{Q}\ \overline{N}\ \overline{A}\ \overline{G}$$

2. Responsible for keeping an accurate record of a trial (two words)

$$\overline{P}\ \overline{B}\ \overline{H}\ \overline{E}\ \overline{G}\qquad \overline{E}\ \overline{R}\ \overline{C}\ \overline{B}\ \overline{E}\ \overline{G}\ \overline{R}\ \overline{E}$$

3. A judge's calendar of cases

$$\overline{Q}\ \overline{B}\ \overline{P}\ \overline{X}\ \overline{R}\ \overline{G}$$

4. Where witches were hanged

$$\overline{F}\ \overline{N}\ \overline{Y}\ \overline{R}\ \overline{Z}$$

5. Process for hearing a case

$$\overline{G}\ \overline{E}\ \overline{V}\ \overline{N}\ \overline{Y}$$

6. Scientific witness

$$\overline{R}\ \overline{K}\ \overline{C}\ \overline{R}\ \overline{E}\ \overline{G}$$

7. Opposite of a not guilty plea (two words)

$$\overline{T}\ \overline{H}\ \overline{V}\ \overline{Y}\ \overline{G}\ \overline{L}\qquad \overline{C}\ \overline{Y}\ \overline{R}\ \overline{N}$$

8. Person claiming a crime happened to him or her

$$\overline{I}\ \overline{V}\ \overline{P}\ \overline{G}\ \overline{V}\ \overline{Z}$$

9. Person who safeguards judge, jury, and witnesses

$$\overline{O}\ \overline{N}\ \overline{V}\ \overline{Y}\ \overline{V}\ \overline{S}\ \overline{S}$$

Name _____ Date _____

Court Word Scrambler

Unscramble these vocabulary words having to do with courts. Use the word bank at the bottom of the page.

1. EDJUG _____

2. TDKCEO _____

3. RUOEORPTSC _____

4. NICMTOALP _____

5. TADEEFNND _____

6. AITLR _____

7. CVREIDT _____

8. TOCRU _____

9. SSSEEITWN _____

10. MCVIIT _____

11. SAWUTIL _____

12. FILBAIF _____

13. ABLEPAIRANG _____

14. NORTYEAT _____

15. CLOCKERFROUT _____

Word Bank

victim	judge	witnesses
attorney	court	prosecutor
jury	complaint	trial
defendant	verdict	docket
bailiff	plea bargain	lawsuit
clerk of court		

Name _____ Date _____

Court Word Search Puzzle

Find the words listed below and circle them in the word search puzzle. Words may be printed in the puzzle forward, backward, horizontally, vertically, or diagonally.

```
N U W S D T R U O C F O K R E L C B M H
P H W I S E R E X N I A G R A B A E L P
V M G G T J F U T V C N Q G I W N R P G
Y W X V R P U E O R T N I A L P M O C N
L P O E U I D V N C O X O T B E H Q V W
A R C R O G U E E S F P M J Q P G N M Q
Y O M D C B A F V N E O E D K D L K T T
W S O I E E L G E Y I A T R U L W V E C
I E O C T X C N X Q V L T P T K T X K C
T C K T A O O A P S K M E T M R F B C N
N U H N L G U G E E F C Q C O E U M O W
E T K A L S R M R N F A T V A R T O D E
S O W D E O T K T T M F M R T T N N C E
S R P N P K S W W E J I I J I T A E O A
T H N E P N Y I I N E H T L D A C S Y C
X J V F A Z S B T C M J Q C I F L L P W
D J L E F F T E N E U T Q J I A K W Q H
R K R D J B E C E Z N H Q O E V B Q K V
H J H F F W M E S M O V G L B J I L R Y
G V Y V D V D A S D G X J U D G E P O X
```

WORD LIST

appellate courts	bailiff	clerk of court
complaint	contempt of court	court reporter
defendant	defense attorney	docket
dual court system	expert witness	judge
juvenile	lay witness	plea bargain
prosecutor	sentence	trial
verdict	victim	

42

Name _____ Date _____

Justice Crossword Puzzle

Use the clues below to complete the crossword puzzle.

ACROSS

2. Decision of a judge or jury
6. The process for hearing a case
7. Defendant admitting he did the crime (two words)
9. Someone charged with a crime
12. Those responsible for enforcing laws
13. _____ courts review the procedures and penalties of trial courts.
15. Deals with the punishments of people convicted of crimes

DOWN

1. Person claiming to be the injured party of a crime
3. Place where a trial is held
4. Place where witch trials were held
5. Person who represents the accused (two words)
8. Person representing the state in a case against a defendant
10. A judge's calendar of cases
11. Federal and state court systems existing side by side (three words)
14. When the defendant pleads "guilty" or "not guilty"

Name _____ Date _____

Justice Word Search Puzzle

Find the words listed below and circle them in the word search puzzle. Words may be printed in the puzzle forward, backward, horizontally, vertically, or diagonally.

```
P  P  Y  A  T  N  E  M  U  G  R  A  G  N  I  S  O  L  C  K
R  J  E  G  W  G  G  V  Y  V  E  R  D  I  C  T  C  O  I  X
E  L  B  V  J  O  N  Z  V  Z  M  D  Y  O  Z  E  C  N  F
L  G  A  L  I  U  W  I  M  R  O  P  F  U  P  P  J  S  V  I
I  S  Z  I  A  D  D  S  K  P  C  P  S  M  E  G  U  L  E  N
M  X  A  N  R  I  E  G  D  O  D  R  S  A  N  N  R  A  S  F
I  J  T  L  G  T  R  N  M  Z  O  O  E  S  I  I  Y  E  T  O
N  U  N  W  E  L  H  T  C  E  E  B  C  S  N  C  D  P  I  R
A  S  E  S  L  M  G  C  I  E  N  A  O  H  G  N  E  P  G  M
R  T  M  A  O  R  W  Z  N  I  U  T  R  Y  A  E  L  A  A  A
Y  I  N  G  L  U  W  I  J  E  W  I  P  S  R  T  I  C  T  T
H  C  G  N  Q  C  D  X  T  S  B  O  E  T  G  N  B  Z  I  I
E  E  I  W  J  K  J  S  U  C  S  N  U  E  U  E  E  T  O  O
A  P  A  F  I  D  S  S  N  E  H  N  D  R  M  S  R  S  N  N
R  R  R  T  B  A  P  U  M  L  J  T  W  I  E  I  A  E  H  X
I  B  R  A  R  E  K  X  Q  B  I  T  R  A  N  S  T  R  Y  E
N  D  A  P  C  C  X  T  W  D  N  M  M  I  T  R  I  R  B  Z
G  S  M  T  L  A  I  R  T  Y  R  U  J  O  A  B  O  A  H  M
N  W  L  H  H  P  A  R  O  L  E  Y  N  Y  L  L  N  E  S  T
I  N  D  I  C  T  M  E  N  T  C  M  E  B  F  S  S  I  S  M
```

WORD LIST

appeals	arraignment	arrest
bench trial	booking	closing argument
due process	evidence	indictment
information	investigation	judgment
jury deliberations	jury trial	justice
mass hysteria	opening argument	parole
preliminary hearing	probation	Salem Witch Trials
sentencing	suspect	trial
verdict		

44

Law Enforcement

Our laws are enforced by police agencies at all three levels of government. Our system of law enforcement has its origins hundreds of years ago with the early efforts of English society to prevent crime, apprehend offenders, and punish the guilty.

England was once divided into *shires* or counties. The chief law enforcement officer of a shire was called a *reeve.* Thus the "shire-reeve" is recognized in the United States as a *sheriff.* Officers working in cities were referred to as *constables.* When either the sheriff or a constable needed help in catching a criminal, he could order local citizens to join in the search. The group they formed was called a *posse.*

The first modern police force was the "Bobbies" of the Metropolitan Police of London.

As English towns grew, the communities depended on the *bailiffs* to keep the peace. These officers were part of a night watch. Their duties included patrolling for thieves, detecting fires, and guarding the city gates. King Edward I (1272–1307) is credited with providing the first police force. Cities were broken down into *wards* or districts Officers assigned to these areas were obliged to patrol or keep *watch.* Hence, the term *watch and ward* was introduced as a way to describe the daily activities of early police officers.

By the early 1700s crime in London had reached new levels. Various reform efforts were made to curb the high rates of violence. It became obvious that the old watch and ward system was outdated. A new approach to crime fighting was needed. Henry Fielding, a writer and *magistrate* (judge) who worked in the Bow Street section of London, had an idea.

Fielding recruited a hand-picked group of officers. Their tasks were to prevent crime and arrest offenders through careful investigation. This disciplined group prided themselves on their rapid response to calls for help; they often dashed to the scene of a crime. Because of the unit's location in metropolitan London and their quick reactions, they became known as the "Bow Street Runners." Some scholars view them as the first detective force.

The person most responsible for single-handedly creating a modern police force is Sir Robert Peel. In 1829 he established the Metropolitan Police of London and introduced radical changes in how the police did their jobs. Peel's officers were nicknamed "Bobbies" by the public in honor of their founder. Bobbies wore uniforms, patrolled the streets, showed discipline and courtesy to citizens, and enforced the laws fairly. The new police force resembled a military system with ranks of office, badges, and weapons. This military-style approach to law enforcement was later adopted in the United States.

Law enforcement has evolved dramatically since Peel's reforms. Some of these changes are technological, including crime labs, patrol cars, radios, computers, fingerprinting techniques, and a national clearinghouse for criminal records. There are over 10,000 police agencies throughout the country that are authorized to enforce the law. The areas and laws that a police agency has authority over are called its *jurisdiction* or domain.

45

Organization of Law Enforcement

Government	Agencies	Jurisdiction
Federal	FBI, Secret Service, IRS, and others	Federal laws and crimes; e.g., counterfeiting
State	Highway patrol, State Bureau of Investigation, and others	State laws and crimes
Local	Sheriff's Departments Municipal Police Depts.	County: State laws and crimes City: State/local laws and crimes

Law enforcement agencies are varied. Public police agencies include:

• over 12,000 city departments.
• 50 federal law enforcement agencies.
• over 1,700 "special police" units such as public housing and university police.
• over 3,000 sheriff's departments.
• 49 state police agencies.
• close to two million persons who work in the private security industry.

There are many duties of a law enforcement officer. An officer must try to prevent crime, enforce laws, protect society, and perform social service functions like helping the elderly. When a person is suspected of committing a crime, he or she is to be arrested by a law enforcement officer. An *arrest* is a detention of someone who must answer for specific charges relating to a crime such as burglary or auto theft. In deciding whom to arrest, a police officer must use discretion (good judgment). Whether or not to arrest a person and what type of charges to give an arrested person are examples of police discretion. An arrested citizen will be sent to court to have his or her case reviewed by a judge or jury. At that point the arresting officer has "handed over" the case and goes back to his daily duties.

Federal Bureau of Investigation

The Federal Bureau of Investigation (FBI) was created in 1908 as a branch of the Department of Justice. It is probably the most well-known of all federal police agencies. FBI agents were once called "G-Men" or "government men." Their early duties were limited to the investigation of a few types of federal crimes. They pursued and caught famous criminals of the 1920s and 1930s such as John Dillinger and Machine Gun Kelly. Since 1908 the U.S. Congress has added up to 281 crimes to the roster of FBI investigations. Several important events mark the growth of the FBI—also known as "The Bureau."

1908—Federal Bureau of Investigation established.
1910—New federal law (White Slave Traffic Act) expanded FBI duties.
1917—Espionage Act enables FBI to study the activities of traitors.
1924—J. Edgar Hoover selected to post of chief executive of the FBI.
    Identification Division created to collect data on crimes.
1930—Uniform Crime Report placed under the FBI's authority.
1932—FBI crime laboratory started.
1935—FBI begins to offer courses and training at its National Academy in Quantico, Virginia.

Early targets of the FBI included members of organized crime gangs.

The FBI has many responsibilities. Among these is the *Uniform Crime Reporting Program (UCR)*. The FBI collects and interprets statistics on various crimes as reported to them by police departments in every state. These crimes are placed in one of two categories: Part 1 (major crimes) or Part 2 (less serious crimes).

A complete account of the crime "picture" in the United States is published yearly by the FBI. It is the only national record of its kind; society depends on the UCR report to get a general idea of crime rates, crime trends, and outcomes of cases.

Since 1908 the Federal Bureau of Investigation has grown tremendously. Over 21,000 people are employed by the Bureau. Field offices are in every state. The FBI's budget exceeds $1 billion annually. This makes it possible for the Bureau to conduct investigations, collect crime data, and operate a laboratory, fingerprint unit, and training academy. For these and other reasons, the FBI remains an important agency in the effort to control crime.

Employment in the FBI

Have you ever wondered what it would take to be hired as a "special agent" or crime fighter for the federal government? Here are two examples of the basic job requirements for the Federal Bureau of Investigation and the Border Patrol.

To join the FBI you must:

1. be between the age of 23 and 27.
2. be in excellent physical health.
3. have uncorrected vision of not less than 20/ 200 correctable to 20/20 in one eye, and at least 20/40 in the other eye.
4. have sound hearing.
5. be a U.S. citizen.
6. have a valid driver's license.
7. agree to a background check.
8. have a college or law degree.
9. pass an initial written exam.
10. have a formal interview.
11. agree to a urinalysis.
12. take a polygraph exam.

By the way—if you are hired as a special agent, the salary is about $33,000 per year. You should expect to be transferred several times during the course of your career before being permanently assigned.

To join the Border Patrol you must:

1. satisfy all of the same requirements as an FBI agent would except #8 above (college or law degree).
2. have some college education.
3. have one year's employment as a supervisor (a bachelor's degree is an acceptable substitute).
4. be fluent in Spanish (reading and speaking).

By the way—a border patrol agent's salary starts off at $18,340 per year. Your first assignment will be in a town somewhere along the Mexican border.

48

Name _____ Date _____

Police Cryptogram

Decipher these words that relate to law enforcement (see page 68 for master key).

1. Seen as the first official detective force (three words)

$\overline{O}\ \overline{B}\ \overline{J}$ $\overline{F}\ \overline{G}\ \overline{E}\ \overline{R}\ \overline{R}\ \overline{G}$ $\overline{E}\ \overline{H}\ \overline{A}\ \overline{A}\ \overline{R}\ \overline{E}\ \overline{F}$

2. The power of police to arrest or not is called

$\overline{Q}\ \overline{V}\ \overline{F}\ \overline{P}\ \overline{E}\ \overline{R}\ \overline{G}\ \overline{V}\ \overline{B}\ \overline{A}$

3. Another term for a judge

$\overline{Z}\ \overline{N}\ \overline{T}\ \overline{V}\ \overline{F}\ \overline{G}\ \overline{E}\ \overline{N}\ \overline{G}\ \overline{R}$

4. Person who created London's Bow Street Runners (two words)

$\overline{U}\ \overline{R}\ \overline{A}\ \overline{E}\ \overline{L}$ $\overline{S}\ \overline{V}\ \overline{R}\ \overline{Y}\ \overline{Q}\ \overline{V}\ \overline{A}\ \overline{T}$

5. The king who provided the first English police force (two words)

$\overline{P}\ \overline{Q}\ \overline{J}\ \overline{N}\ \overline{E}\ \overline{Q}$ $\overline{V}$

6. Areas and laws over which a police agency has authority

$\overline{W}\ \overline{H}\ \overline{E}\ \overline{V}\ \overline{F}\ \overline{Q}\ \overline{V}\ \overline{P}\ \overline{G}\ \overline{V}\ \overline{B}\ \overline{A}$

7. A police detention of someone suspected of committing a crime

$\overline{N}\ \overline{E}\ \overline{E}\ \overline{R}\ \overline{F}\ \overline{G}$

8. Former nickname for FBI agents (two words)

$\overline{T}\ \overline{-}\ \overline{Z}\ \overline{R}\ \overline{A}$

9. Crime information collected yearly by the FBI (three words)

$\overline{H}\ \overline{A}\ \overline{V}\ \overline{S}\ \overline{B}\ \overline{E}\ \overline{Z}$ $\overline{P}\ \overline{E}\ \overline{V}\ \overline{Z}\ \overline{R}$ $\overline{E}\ \overline{R}\ \overline{C}\ \overline{B}\ \overline{E}\ \overline{G}\ \overline{F}$

10. Former Chief Executive of the FBI (three words)

$\overline{W}$ $\overline{R}\ \overline{Q}\ \overline{T}\ \overline{N}\ \overline{E}$ $\overline{U}\ \overline{B}\ \overline{B}\ \overline{I}\ \overline{R}\ \overline{E}$

Name _____ Date _____

Police Word Scrambler

Unscramble these police words. Use the word bank at the bottom of the page.

1. AFIFBLI _____

2. BBBSOEI _____

3. ESOPS _____

4. EEEEVHRSRI _____

5. TERARS _____

6. RTEORELEBP _____

7. GFNIELDI _____

8. SDIIIOCJTNRU _____

9. TMTGRSEAAI _____

10. RNTAAWR _____

11. OVORHE _____

12. BAILI _____

13. BLASTCONES _____

14. FREFISH _____

15. RUDESPOCES _____

Word Bank

Hoover	due process	alibi
Bobbies	magistrate	posse
jurisdiction	shire reeve	sheriff
Fielding	arrest	Robert Peel
warrant	bailiff	constables

Name _____ Date _____

Police Word Search

Find the words listed below and circle them in the word search puzzle. Words may be printed in the puzzle forward, backward, horizontally, vertically, or diagonally.

```
U F C B N C P Y E W O E W M J V D U W J
N Y D C O G L Y R E V O O H R A G D E J
I V N O J D R A W D N A H C T A W Y P W
F N G N F B A A D I S C R E T I O N J A
O O T S P C C S E C R E T S E R V I C E
R I P T G F U N Y F F I L I A B J N A G
M T K A P U A M W W J X O G G D P G V F
C C F B A R O B E R T P E E L G M F M P
R I U L L O R T A P Y A W H G I H I B F
I D O E U H T K R H C D Y Q F T Z G N F
M S P J E H J N T V L T X U B E - W Z V
E I E C S R F P O S S E R O N M Y S F S
R R D A R R E S T T A Z B I E L H J V Q
E U W B O I W C Q Z C B L N T E M W O S
P J A E L L E G J U I A H P R W T F E P
O N R R S P P V J E Y U E I Y Q L I S B
R M D I S N T K S K T H F V O J J Z P P
T A I U L Q A D A I W F B K T O H B I O
D M S G B O W S T R E E T R U N N E R S
C T X K H E N R Y F I E L D I N G V R P
```

WORD LIST

arrest

Bow Street Runners

Edward I

Henry Fielding

jurisdiction

secret service

Uniform Crime Report

bailiff

constable

FBI

highway patrol

posse

sheriff

watch and ward

Bobbies

discretion

G-Men

J. Edgar Hoover

Robert Peel

suspect

Name _____ Date _____

Police Crossword Puzzle

Use the clues below to complete the crossword puzzle.

ACROSS

1. Language one must speak to be in the Border Patrol
3. J. Edgar Hoover was director of this agency.
7. Chief law officer of English counties (two words)
9. Father of modern policing (three words)
14. Fielding's officers who ran to crime scenes (three words)

DOWN

2. Citizens "rounded up" to help catch a crook
4. Officer who kept watch in early English times
5. Nickname for London police
6. Early system of law enforcement (three words)
8. When police take someone into custody
10. Early form of judge
11. The FBI is a part of the Department of _____ .
12. The areas and laws that a police agency has authority over
13. _____ police departments are responsible for law enforcement in cities.
15. This act enabled the FBI to investigate traitors (two words).

Extent of Crime

In order to reduce and prevent crime we must collect basic facts or data about the nature of crime in the United States. This information helps us to answer the following questions regarding criminal activities:

1. How much crime is there? This is known as crime *frequency*.
2. Where and when do these crimes occur? This refers to the *distribution* of offenses throughout the nation.
3. What types of crimes are committed? This requires the placing of crimes into categories or *typologies* (a way of organizing data).
4. Who are the offenders? This pertains to a *classification* of criminals based on age, gender, race, and other factors.

Purse-snatching falls under the crime category of larceny.

Each month, the Federal Bureau of Investigation collects information on crimes reported to them from over 15,000 police agencies. The results are published in the *Uniform Crime Reports* (UCR). The UCR gives us a general set of answers to the questions listed above. From these answers we can create a picture of the crime problem.

The FBI divides the statistics it receives each month into one of two categories. Each category contains a group of major crimes. *Part I Offenses* are composed of eight types of crimes the FBI believes to be the most serious and most likely to be ably reported. These are called the *index crimes* and consist of robbery, aggravated assault, forcible rape, motor vehicle theft, arson, criminal homicide, and burglary. Like a thermometer, we use these index crimes to point out changes in the number of offenses happening from year to year. Twenty-one other crimes make up the category of *Part II Offenses,* such as simple assault and fraud. Although these crimes are usually less severe in nature, information on Part II Offenses is helpful in studying the extent of crime.

A second source of official measures of crimes is the *National Crime Survey* (NCS). Over 45,000 households are sampled. Each is surveyed as to whether or not they have been the victims of crime. If so, the NCS collects detailed information about each experience or activity. Only six types of crimes are incorporated in the NCS—rape, robbery, assault, larceny, burglary, and motor vehicle theft. NCS reports show that people are victimized far more often than are reported to the police. There is, in other words, a big gap between the rate of victimization and the rate of crimes shown in the Uniform Crime Report.

One last method for evaluating crime is the *self-report survey.* People are asked to discuss their own criminal actions. The answers are recorded in an anonymous survey or interview. This method looks at crimes committed by average citizens in order to uncover the hidden or unreported rates of crime. A self-report survey provides us with a fresh and different perspective on the crime "picture."

Crime Facts

• Murder rates peak in the summer and occur more often in the South. The killer is usually a male, between the ages of 18 and 24, and probably a friend or family member of the victim. The preferred choice of weapon remains the firearm.

• Males traditionally commit the majority of crimes, with a few exceptions such as shoplifting and welfare fraud.

• Offenders begin to "drop out" of crime permanently starting at roughly the age of 30. This is known as the "aging out process" by which some people choose to quit the life of crime.

• Burglary is a Part I Offense that has shown a significant decrease in the past 15 years. Fewer burglaries, for reasons unknown, are occurring.

• Larceny (theft) appears to be the most frequently-occurring major crime in the country. Larceny includes activities such as shoplifting, purse-snatching, and property theft.

• Over 1.5 million motor vehicles were reported stolen to the police in 1992. This includes autos, boats, buses, trucks, and motorcycles.

• Young males—not women or children—are most often the victims of crime.

• Public opinion polls reveal that citizens are greatly afraid of being harmed by strangers. The truth is that we are more likely to be harmed by friends or family members.

• The FBI operates a *crime clock* that explains the crime rates by type and time across the country. For instance:

     -one burglary every 11 seconds
     -one robbery every 47 seconds
     -one violent crime every 22 seconds
     -one motor vehicle theft every 20 seconds

• About 25 percent of all American families/households are affected by crime, either as victims, witnesses, or offenders.

• Overall crime rates continue to be significantly higher in cities than in rural areas. The prospect of becoming a victim is also higher in cities.

• Gang murders continue to rise—in Los Angeles in 1991, over 700 people were killed in gang-related murders.

Did You Know?

- In the early 1900s New York City was plagued by violent gangs with unusual names like the "Dead Rabbits," the "Plug Uglies," and the "Hudson Dusters."

- We spend over $75 billion for the services of the police, courts, and prisons.

- The police recorded over 12 million arrests in 1992.

- Over 1.6 million people are in correctional facilities like prisons and jails.

- Juveniles have no constitutional right to a jury trial. Also, juveniles can be searched in school without a warrant or good reason by the police.

- Males have an overall arrest ratio of 4 to 1 compared to females.

- Crime rates are almost always highest during the summertime.

- Thurgood Marshall was the first black citizen appointed to serve as a member of the U.S. Supreme Court (1967–1991).

- In 1910 Alice Stebbins Wells became the first female to be appointed to the position of police officer with arrest powers.

- About 17,000 law enforcement agencies exist in the United States.

- Felony courts process over 1.5 million cases involving serious crimes yearly.

- Every year, our courts review and handle in excess of 100 million cases that include civil, traffic, and criminal cases.

- No two states have identical sets of criminal laws.

- One robbery occurs every 47 seconds somewhere in the United States.

- Violent crimes occur in the greatest numbers during hot weather.

- At one time it was believed that one could identify criminals solely on the basis of their physical appearance. This was known as the school of biological positivism, or the belief that offenders had a different "look" from law-abiding citizens.

- Over 50,000 women are currently housed in federal and state prisons around the country.

- There are over 2,700 inmates on death row; only the federal government and 38 states, however, use the death penalty.

            55

Name _____ Date _____

Crime Picture Word Scrambler

Unscramble these words that relate to the crime picture. Use the word bank at the bottom of the page if you need to.

1. FRIESTRNUICMRRMEOPO _____

2. YYOOLGPT _____

3. REICM _____

4. BOBRERY _____

5. IFB _____

6. ECMRIKLCOC _____

7. ARLNEYC _____

8. XINEDSMCIRE _____

9. QUEECYNFR _____

10. LESF-ROPRET _____

11. CELANYEVRANIMIROUST _____

12. TSSAAUL _____

13. RUREDM _____

14. TAPRNEO _____

15. ISRIUTONDTBI _____

Word Bank

Distribution	part one	Uniform Crime Reports
typology	murder	crime
robbery	assault	FBI
crime clock	self-report	National Crime Survey
larceny	index crimes	frequency

Name _____ Date _____

Crime Word Search Puzzle

Find the words listed below and circle them in the word search puzzle. Words may be printed in the puzzle forward, backward, horizontally, vertically, or diagonally.

```
Y S O S W T E M G O V O M W K V C P D E
B E T L E M P H Y N W Y G O L O P Y T P
P T V R I M J A H C Z J A J Z C X I Y H
P Y P R O Y I C R T N A Q U W X H A G V
O U C A U P K R R T R E R U P L K X Y F
F B I D R S E T C I I O U L Z H T Z N Z
F G K I R T E R W X M I P Q D W T E E J
F P P S V T I M E O E E O E E F M S C W
W A E T I V P O I M D D C F R R K H R O
F S I R R W B Q F R I M N L F - F W A T
L S J I S E S D V F C R Y I O E F N L P
K A G B W D D V Y L E L C R B C N L P P
A U G U V V H R T R S N A M E U K S E R
J L R T B M W R U Z A I S N R B Q S E S
K T Q I D U A R F M A L Z E O O B D D S
B G K O G X Q O J F E Y G Z S I F O G X
V H B N E B G K C G J I U R I D T I R I
N O I T A C I F I S S A L C U S W A N F
O N S Z L O Q B A C C A R E J B A Q N U
B I O L O G I C A L P O S I T I V I S M
```

WORD LIST

assault	biological positivism	burglary
classification	crime	crime clock
distribution	FBI	fraud
frequency	index crimes	larceny
murder	National Crime Survey	Part I Offenses
Part II Offenses	robbery	self-report
typology	Uniform Crime Reports	

Explaining Criminal Behavior

Scholars have long sought to answer the question "What is the cause of criminal behavior?" Why, for instance, do some people steal cars or rob banks? Over the past century, a number of thoughtful explanations or theories were formed to address this question. A *theory* is a broad idea or set of ideas that seeks to explain a very complex problem or issue. These theories of crime can be placed within various *schools of thought. Criminology* refers to the study of criminal behavior.

The *classical* school of criminology is based on two fundamental ideas about crime. First, people break the law because they choose to do so, acting of their own *free will*. Second,

The sociological school of criminology states that peer pressure and other external factors may be causes for criminal behavior.

crime can be prevented by punishing an offender severely enough to outweigh any rewards for his actions. For example, if someone steals $100, the correct penalty would be a fine of $100. This principle of punishment is sometimes referred to as "just desserts," or getting what one deserves for breaking the law.

The *biological* school of criminology looks at physical or "internal" causes of crime. Some believe that people may inherit a criminal gene from their parents. Others argue that low intelligence, poor diet, or a damaged brain could contribute to criminal behavior. In any case, the biological approach views treatment, not punishment, as a possible cure for lawbreakers. This school also says that criminals may have a physical appearance that is different from other members of society.

A final perspective is the *sociological* school of criminology. People in this school believe that crimes are committed because of peer pressure, such as pressure to join a gang. Also, the lack of personal restraints in some will lead them into crime; they cannot resist the chance to break the law. A few people learn to be offenders. Their family, community, or lifestyle may teach them to embrace a criminal lifestyle. Thus, according to this viewpoint, entire families of criminals may develop over time. Also, poor living conditions and lack of jobs may encourage some persons to resort to crime as one way to achieve a feeling of success.

It is worth noting that no single theory can fully and accurately describe the many cases of crime. People break the law for a variety of reasons. To date, we have been unable to show a definite cause-effect relationship. Poverty, for instance, may contribute to the crime problem, but most low-income families do not participate in crimes. We should accept theories as directional signals pointing us closer to uncovering the roots of crime rather than absolute answers to our question of "why." Once we discover the reasons for crime we may begin our search for practical solutions.

Name _____ Date _____

Why Did She Do It?

Lola is a 36-year-old elementary school teacher. She has a husband, three children, two cats, and a dog named Mocha. Life has been good to Lola, especially on her last birthday when she was notified that she had inherited several million dollars from an elderly woman she had barely known.

The day after she received the money, she paid off all her debts and then bought presents for her family. Still, there was over $8 million left to be spent.

Exactly one week after receiving her inheritance, Lola purchased a revolver and robbed the First Federal Bank. Her "haul" amounted to $5,321. She was arrested 20 minutes later while ordering lunch at a diner across from the bank.

When asked why someone so rich would want to rob a bank, Lola shrugged her shoulders and replied, "Whatever!"

So, why did she do it? Write out a possible theory that might explain Lola's behavior.

_____

_____

_____

_____

_____

_____

_____

_____

_____

_____

_____

_____

_____

_____

Name _____ Date _____

Criminal Behavior Word Scrambler

Unscramble these words that relate to criminal behavior. Use the word bank if you need to.

1. YOETHR _____

2. EAIRBHVO _____

3. SSUEAC _____

4. RMNLGCIIOOY _____

5. OLUCOHGOHTHSTOF _____

6. CAILASCLS _____

7. NMLCRIIA _____

8. EFERLIWL _____

9. OIOIAGLLBC _____

10. OIOIOAGLLSCC _____

11. FEETLLIYS _____

12. MATTERTEN _____

13. DRAWERS _____

14. FERNSDOFE _____

15. EREPSEEPRURS _____

Word Bank

peer pressure	sociological	classical
criminology	rewards	offenders
causes	school of thought	criminal
biological	behavior	treatment
free will	lifestyle	theory

Name _____ Date _____

Criminal Behavior Word Search Puzzle

Find the words listed below and circle them in the word search puzzle. Words may be printed in the puzzle forward, backward, horizontally, vertically, or diagonally.

```
J  E  P  X  T  N  E  M  T  A  E  R  T  H  E  O  R  Y  R  K
N  Y  H  K  B  V  Z  Z  B  E  F  L  N  T  I  P  C  R  D  R
K  G  Y  Y  T  R  E  V  O  P  Q  P  A  H  S  R  D  K  J  O
X  O  S  V  X  Z  Z  M  B  E  V  E  G  G  K  N  R  M  A  I
E  L  I  Y  M  C  P  E  J  R  J  R  N  U  D  D  V  Y  I  V
J  O  C  C  N  L  R  L  E  U  F  S  D  O  E  E  M  Y  P  A
Q  N  A  V  C  A  A  A  L  S  Z  O  N  H  P  S  K  L  T  H
P  I  L  S  K  S  Q  C  L  S  U  N  E  T  I  T  E  K  N  E
R  M  A  O  D  S  X  I  S  E  J  A  L  F  Q  R  N  C  M  B
F  I  P  C  H  I  M  G  O  R  S  L  Y  O  Q  E  E  E  N  L
R  R  P  I  C  C  E  O  T  P  K  R  T  S  X  S  G  F  E  A
E  C  E  O  R  A  R  L  N  R  I  E  S  L  Y  S  L  C  S  N
E  P  A  L  J  L  Z  O  E  E  Q  S  E  O  A  E  A  U  U  I
W  O  R  O  R  R  K  I  M  E  P  T  F  O  B  D  N  G  O  M
I  O  A  G  P  O  Z  B  H  P  G  R  I  H  Y  T  I  I  S  I
L  R  N  I  O  L  Y  U  S  X  L  A  L  C  B  S  M  O  M  R
L  D  C  C  F  B  R  E  I  D  W  I  L  S  X  U  I  Q  T  C
H  I  E  A  I  V  O  O  N  X  J  N  A  Z  Y  J  R  P  O  Z
Z  E  H  L  A  X  V  V  U  S  W  T  G  U  O  W  C  N  A  I
P  T  C  A  U  S  E  S  P  L  V  S  H  S  D  R  A  W  E  R
```

WORD LIST

biological	causes	classical
criminal behavior	criminal gene	criminology
free will	just desserts	lifestyle
peer pressure	personal restraints	physical appearance
poor diet	poverty	punishment
rewards	schools of thought	sociological
theory	treatment	

61

Juvenile Justice

There is a separate system of justice for children. Youth who get into trouble with the law are called *delinquents.* They are brought to a juvenile court and initially placed under the direct supervision of a juvenile *probation officer.* This officer is responsible for a variety of duties. These include investigating the charges, assisting children in need, and helping the court make a "good" decision about what to do with a juvenile.

A delinquency *petition* is a request for the court to review the actions of a child to decide if he is a delinquent. The *hearing* is conducted to review the evidence. A judge's decision that a child is indeed a delinquent is called an *adjudication.* There are many options available to a judge. He may order the delinquent to be sent to a training school or *reformatory* for a period of time. Also, the youth may be placed on *probation*, given a *foster home,* put on *house arrest,* or sent to a special program. Children who drink alcohol or take drugs are often sent to clinics or halfway houses to receive intensive treatment for their problems.

Temptations to use drugs, steal, or join gangs are faced by young people every day. Juveniles who break the law because of these and other illegal activities are called delinquents.

The goal of juvenile justice is to keep children out of trouble. A priority of the courts is to find ways to help rather than punish delinquents. Much like a loving parent, the judge is concerned with the long-term welfare of children in his custody. Juveniles who commit serious crimes (felonies), however, may be *transferred* to the adult judicial system to stand trial. Each state has a minimum age at which juveniles become eligible for transfer. A juvenile who stands trial for a serious crime may receive adult penalties ranging from a brief period of imprisonment to a death sentence. Most juveniles, however, stay within the juvenile court. They are classified by information based on their past behavior; every child fits into one or more categories defined by law.

There are many categories of juvenile classification. *Dependent* juveniles have no one to care for them. The state must provide food, clothing, and other needs for these youth. *Neglected* or *abused* children are placed under state care because their parents hurt or ignored them.

Delinquents are the chief concern of the juvenile justice system. These are children who break the law, causing harm to people and property. Some do things that are considered "adult crimes" but are not sent to adult court. *Status offenders,* on the other hand, break rules and regulations such as not going to school. Such actions are illegal for minors but not for adults. A final type of delinquent is the *incorrigible child.* He or she has been labeled unmanageable or "out of control" by the court.

Delinquents come from all types of families and neighborhoods. Usually their involvement with crime is limited to property and drug-related offenses. Many of these delinquents will spend a portion of their adolescence on probation or in a juvenile facility. It is the duty of the juvenile court to help these children.

Legal Rights of Juveniles

• Students and their property may be searched on school grounds by school officials if there is "reasonable suspicion" against them.

• A juvenile being formally processed by the juvenile court shall have access to an attorney who will assist him or her.

• A juvenile is considered innocent until proven guilty beyond a reasonable doubt.

• Juveniles have the right not to say something that would incriminate them in court.

• A court must provide a timely, full notice to the juvenile of all the charges brought against him or her.

• Arrested juveniles have the right to face and cross-examine witnesses during a delinquency hearing.

• Juveniles do not automatically have a right to a trial by jury in juvenile court. That particular decision is up to the judge.

• Juveniles convicted of murders committed at age 16 or 17 may be given the death penalty in states adhering to capital punishment.

• All juveniles are entitled to an adequate standard of living and care.

• Juvenile delinquents have the right to "reasonable" treatment and rehabilitation.

• Ordinarily a juvenile may request that the press and public be barred from attending his hearing.

• Juvenile delinquents have a right to be safe from cruel and unusual punishments by the state.

"A state in all its dealings must, of course, accord every person due process of law. And due process may require that some of the same restrictions which the Constitution has placed upon criminal trials must be imposed upon juvenile proceedings."

In Re Gault, 1967
United States Supreme Court

Name _____ Date _____

Juvenile Justice Cryptogram

Decipher these words that relate to juvenile justice (see page 68 for master key).

1. Request for a court to decide if a child is a delinquent

C R G V G V B A

2. Juveniles in trouble with the law

Q R Y V A D H R A G

3. A judge's decision to label a child as delinquent

N Q W H Q V P N G V B A

4. Juvenile offender sent to adult court

G E N A F S R E

5. Children who have no one to care for them

Q R C R A Q R A G

6. Those who commit actions that are illegal for minors but not for adults

F G N G H F   B S S R A Q R E F

7. A child labeled as "out of control"

V A P B E E V T V O Y R

8. Person in charge of supervising delinquent

C E B O N G V B A   B S S V P R E

9. A _____ is held to review the evidence about a delinquent

U R N E V A T

10. _____ children are ignored by their parents

A R T Y R P G R Q

Name _____ Date _____

Juvenile Justice Word Scrambler

Unscramble these words that relate to juvenile justice. Use the word bank if you need to.

1. TTIIPEON _____

2. NGETDELCE _____

3. NOSTUFAFTRESED _____

4. INQDELTNEU _____

5. SNARTREF _____

6. ERAGHIN _____

7. AFIORPTNFCBROEIO _____

8. DUICJADTNIOA _____

9. PEDEDENNT _____

10. BGLERRCNIIIO _____

11. RECREATSFO _____

12. LINEVUEJ _____

13. FARMROOTYER _____

14. HAHAFLOSYUWE _____

15. SUBADE _____

Word Bank

incorrigible	petition	dependent
abused	adjudication	juvenile
halfway house	probation officer	delinquent
foster care	hearing	transfer
neglected	status offender	reformatory

Name _____ Date _____

Juvenile Justice Word Search Puzzle

Find the words listed below and circle them in the word search puzzle. Words may be printed in the puzzle forward, backward, horizontally, vertically, or diagonally.

```
Y  N  J  U  F  K  H  P  P  G  T  P  P  A  I  T  O  T  U  F
R  P  V  D  U  H  P  P  G  N  F  F  F  D  N  W  H  C  S  K
H  E  R  W  K  K  O  C  Z  I  N  Q  H  J  E  F  B  A  O  O
O  I  A  O  K  A  H  T  V  R  R  Q  K  U  G  R  Q  P  N  Z
U  S  N  S  B  Z  J  D  N  A  U  I  S  D  L  A  G  I  O  Y
S  R  P  C  O  A  R  Q  Z  E  R  D  S  I  E  D  M  T  I  L
E  E  V  J  O  N  T  E  O  H  U  Y  W  C  C  O  Z  A  T  L
A  D  J  C  G  R  A  I  F  C  Y  Q  F  A  T  L  G  L  A  N
R  N  I  L  J  N  R  B  O  S  L  E  N  T  E  E  H  P  T  O
R  E  F  A  K  I  E  I  L  N  N  F  Z  I  D  S  T  U  I  I
E  F  O  C  B  K  J  O  G  E  O  A  C  O  L  C  K  N  L  T
S  F  S  G  A  U  L  I  F  I  S  F  R  N  B  E  Z  I  I  A
T  O  T  I  K  M  S  W  K  E  B  U  F  T  Q  N  D  S  B  B
P  S  E  U  Y  U  M  E  H  N  W  L  S  I  C  C  G  H  A  O
H  U  R  X  W  R  M  L  D  E  B  R  E  P  C  E  M  M  H  R
J  T  H  W  D  E  P  E  N  D  E  N  T  C  I  E  L  E  E  P
Q  A  O  Q  W  G  V  I  M  O  M  G  O  X  H  C  R  N  R  E
I  T  M  R  N  R  N  O  I  T  I  T  E  P  A  I  I  T  L  F
G  S  E  D  Y  R  O  T  A  M  R  O  F  E  R  G  L  O  T  S
F  U  G  J  U  V  E  N  I  L  E  C  O  U  R  T  K  D  N  U
```

WORD LIST

abused	adjudication	adolescence
capital punishment	delinquent	dependent
foster home	hearing	house arrest
incorrigible child	juvenile court	neglected
petition	probation	probation officer
reasonable suspicion	reformatory	rehabilitation
status offenders	transfer	

Name _____ Date _____

Big 35 Word Search Review

Find the words listed below and circle them in the word search puzzle. Words may be printed in the puzzle forward, backward, horizontally, vertically, or diagonally.

```
S R T N E M N R E V O G E W Y X L L K E
N O E N O I T U T I T S N O C J C S V Q
O T C Q K V T E M Y C A R C O M E D R Q
I U N J W I N Q F K Q Z C I V I L L A W
T C A M A Q I U F J Q F S O O D W E T H
C E N E L T A A I Z W A L F O E L U R O
E S I C L A L L T R O N A E M E D S I M
R O D I A Y P I N F E X E C U T I V E W
R R R L N P M T I C L F Z Z L A I R T I
O P O O I M O Y A Q J U S T I C E T T B
C S L P M A C Z L L Z E B N V L L N I E
K E K W I T A C P Y K H K X U V A A U L
F Q U B R A D L A R E D E F D S I D S B
C C J J C Y J U V E N I L E S J C N W M
O B R E P R E S E N T A T I O N I E A A
U I B T C I D R E V D J U D G E D F L E
R J F Y E V I T A L S I G E L O U E W R
T N F R E E D O M F L O C A L I J D U P
S R X S T N E M D N E M A T E T A T S H
C Q U D U E P R O C E S S T H G I R T M
```

WORD LIST

amendments	civil law	complaint	Constitution
corrections	courts	criminal law	defendant
democracy	due process	equality	executive
federal	felony	freedom	government
judge	judicial	justice	juveniles
lawsuit	legislative	local	misdemeanor
ordinance	plaintiff	police	preamble
prosecutor	representation	rights	rule of law
state	trial	verdict	

Cryptograms: Master Key

Use this master key to decipher the cryptogram activities.

A = N	N = A
B = O	O = B
C = P	P = C
D = Q	Q = D
E = R	R = E
F = S	S = F
G = T	T = G
H = U	U = H
I = V	V = I
J = W	W = J
K = X	X = K
L = Y	Y = L
M = Z	Z = M